The Bonhoeffer Legacy:
An International Journal

The Bonhoeffer Legacy: An International Journal
Volume 6, Issue 1 2018

The Bonhoeffer Legacy: An International Journal is a fully refereed academic journal aimed principally at providing an outlet for an ever expanding Bonhoeffer scholarship in Australia, New Zealand and the South Pacific region, as well as being open to article submissions from Bonhoeffer scholars throughout the world. It also aims to elicit and encourage future and ongoing scholarship in the field. The focus of the journal, captured in the notion of 'Legacy', is on any aspect of Bonhoeffer's life, theology and political action that is relevant to his immense contribution to twentieth century events and scholarship. 'Legacy' can be understood as including those events and ideas that contributed to Bonhoeffer's own development, those that constituted his own context or those that have developed since his time as a result of his work. The editors encourage and welcome any scholarship that contributes to the journal's aims. The journal also has book reviews.

Subscription Rates

Print	On-line	Print and On-line
Aus $65 Individuals	Aus $55 individuals	Aus $75 individuals
Aus $90 Institutions	Aus $80 individuals	Aus $100 instiutions

The Bonhoeffer Legacy: An International Journal is published by ATF Theology an imprint of ATF (Australia) Ltd (ABN 90 116 359 963) and is published once a year.
ISSN 2202-9168

978-1-925612-21-9	soft
978-1-925612-22-6	hard
978-1-925612-23-3	epub
978-1-925612-24-0	pdf

This periodical is indexed in the ATLA Religion Database® (ATLA RDB®), a product of the American Theological Library Association.
Email: atla@atla.com<mailto:atla@atla.com>, www: http://www.atla.com<http://www.atla.com/>.

www.atfpress.com

The Bonhoeffer Legacy:
An International Journal

Adelaide
2018

Vol 6 No 1/2018

Contents

Bibliography

The Dietrich Bonhoeffer Works (English)

General Editors: Victoria Barnett, Wayne Whitson Floyd Jr., and Barbara Wojhoski.

Originally published in German as *Dietrich Bonhoeffer Werke*. Edited by Eberhard Bethge et al. Munich: Chr. Kaiser Verlag, 1986–1998.

DBWE 1   *Sanctorum Communio: A Theological Study of the Sociology of the Church*. Edited by Clifford J. Green. Translated by Reinhard Krauss and Nancy Lukens. Minneapolis: Fortress, 1998.

DBWE 2   *Act and Being: Transcendental Philosophy and Ontology in Systematic Theology*. Edited by Wayne Whitson Floyd, Jr. Translated by H. Martin Rumscheidt. Minneapolis: Fortress, 1998.

DBWE 3   *Creation and Fall: A Theological Exposition of Genesis 1–3*. Edited by John W. de Gruchy. Translated by Douglas Stephen Bax. Minneapolis: Fortress, 1997.

DBWE 4   *Discipleship*. Edited by Geffrey B. Kelly and John D. Godsey. Translated by Barbara Green and Reinhard Krauss. Minneapolis: Fortress, 2001.

DBWE 5   *Life Together; Prayerbook of the Bible*. Edited by Geffrey B. Kelly. Translated by Daniel W. Bloesch and James H. Burtness. Minneapolis: Fortress, 1996.

DBWE 6   *Ethics*. Edited by Clifford J. Green. Translated by Reinhard Krauss, Charles C. West and Douglas W. Stott. Minneapolis: Fortress, 2005.

DBWE 7   *Fiction from Tegel Prison.* Edited by Clifford Green. Translated by Nancy Lukens. Minneapolis: Fortress, 2000.

DBWE 8   *Letters and Papers from Prison.* Edited by John de Gruchy. Translated by Reinhard Krauss and Nancy Lukens.Minneapolis: Fortress, 2010.

DBWE 9   *The Young Bonhoeffer: 1918–1927.* Edited by Paul Duane Matheny, Clifford J. Green and Marshall D. Johnson. Translated by Mary C. Nebelsick and Douglas W. Stott. Minneapolis: Fortress, 2002.

DBWE 10   *Barcelona, Berlin, New York.* Edited by Clifford J. Green. Translated by Douglas W. Stott. Minneapolis: Fortress, 2008.

DBWE 11   *Ecumenical, Academic, and Pastoral Work: 1931–1932.* Edited by Victoria J. Barnett, Mark S. Brocker and Michael B. Lukens. Translated by Anne Schmidt-Lange, Isabel Best, Nicolas Humphrey, Marion Pauck and Douglas W. Stott. Minneapolis: Fortress, 2012.

DBWE 12   *Berlin: 1932–1933.* Edited by Larry L. Rasmussen. Translated by Isabel Best. Minneapolis: Fortress, 2009.

DBWE 13   *London: 1933–1935.* Edited by Keith W. Clements. Translated by Isabel Best. Minneapolis: Fortress, 2007.

DBWE 14   *Theological Education Finkenwalde: 1935–1937.* Edited by Victoria J. Barnett. Translated by Peter Frick. Minneapolis: Fortress, 2011.

DBWE 15   *Theological Education Underground: 1937–1940.* Edited by Victoria J. Barnett. Translated by Claudia D. Bergmann and Peter Frick. Minneapolis: Fortress, 2011.

DBWE 16   *Conspiracy and Imprisonment: 1940–1945.* Edited by Mark S. Brocker. Translated by Lisa E. Dahill. Minneapolis: Fortress, 2006.

DBWE 17   *Indexes and Supplementary Materials.* Edited by Victoria J. Barnett and Barbara Wojhoski. Minneapolis: Fortress, 2014.

Vol 6 No 1/2018

Editorial

The Bonhoeffer Legacy: An International Journal, now in its sixth volume, was initiated principally to provide an outlet for an ever-expanding Bonhoeffer scholarship in Australia, New Zealand and the South Pacific region, one that has included an annual conference since 2004 and a range of symposia and other events called from time to time by Bonhoeffer scholars and interested parties. The initial aim was to support and encourage this extant scholarship from the Australasian region as well as to forge links with and draw into the region the wider and ever-expanding Bonhoeffer scholarship to be found internationally. The international links have grown significantly during the past six years, indicated by an increasing authorship in and subscriptions to the journal coming from all parts of the world. As a result, the Editorial Board made the decision a year ago to re-name the journal slightly, with a new sub-title, *An International Journal*, that captures this reality.

The focus of the journal, seen in the notion of 'Legacy', remains on any aspect of Bonhoeffer's life, theology and/or political action that is relevant to his immense contribution to twentieth and twenty-first century events and scholarship. 'Legacy' can be understood to include those events and ideas that contributed to Bonhoeffer's own development, those that constituted his own context or those that have developed since his time as a result of his work and the many commentaries on it. In other words, Bonhoeffer's legacy can be traced back to the events, philosophies and theologies that preceded his time as well as drawn forward to help in understanding the world we inhabit today, especially around issues of faith, non-faith and the ethics entailed in human action.

In this first issue of the sixth volume, we have a variety of Australian and international scholars whose work illustrates yet again the richness and diversity of the Bonhoeffer legacy. The first article by Keith Clements explores Bonhoeffer's wisdom for ministry in a post-Christian world; it is essentially his public address at the University of Divinity, Melbourne, Australia, early in 2019, which focussed on Bonhoeffer's ongoing relevance in a world that has changed so much since his time. The second article by Dianne Rayson picks up on some of the Clements strands in investigating Bonhoeffer's contribution to consideration of eco-theological and eco-ethical matters, again issues of burning importance to the contemporary world. The third article by John Moses looks to more historical matters in reviewing Bonhoeffer's position on the Jewish question in the time of the Reich. Article four by Derek Taylor explores what the author describes as authentic theological knowledge, a stance rather than mere formulations, as exposed in his reading of *Life Together*. Finally, Peter Truasheim, a two-time winner of the Flechtheim Scholarship for student work that furthers understanding of Bonhoeffer, examines the implications of Bonhoeffer's natural and sacramental theologies in his critique of Barth's 'positivism of revelation' and differences with Brunner.

As we continue to suggest, Bonhoeffer's theology is akin to the unfinished symphony and so possesses an unusual capacity to be taken in any number of directions and to continue to stimulate new theological, ethical and indeed political thought. The Bonhoeffer legacy is unusual in its capacity to take us back to some of the most ancient of theological considerations as well as sharpen our attention to issues alive at the present time.

Terence Lovat
Newcastle, Australia
November, 2019

Vol 6 No 1/2018

Life Together, Life for Others: Dietrich Bonhoeffer's Wisdom for Ministry in a Post-Christian World

Keith Clements

(From a public lecture of 4 February 2019, Whitley College, University of Divinity, Melbourne, Australia)

Introduction

This day, 4 February, is a very fitting date on which to speak about Dietrich Bonhoeffer, for it is his birthday. It is not however his actual birth in 1906 that I suggest we first commemorate; rather, his thirtieth birthday party, on 4 February 1936. This took place in a village called Finkenwalde close to the Baltic coast of north-east Germany. There, an old school was now home to an illegal, underground seminary for training pastors for the Confessing Church, that is, that section of German Protestantism which was resisting the take-over of the Church as an instrument of the Nazi state. The seminary had been formed the previous year, 1935, and Dietrich Bonhoeffer—not yet thirty years old—had been appointed its Director.

Life in such a seminary at such a grim time in Germany was obviously a serious affair. But it was not all work and no play (Australians in particular may be interested to note that on his visits to English theological colleges during 1933–35 Bonhoeffer had been struck by the importance of sports and games in those communities. Consequently, ball games of various kinds were encouraged and popular at Finkenwalde, though not, as far as we know, cricket); and also on the lighter side birthday celebrations were highlights. So it was on this particular evening, as the students and their Director gathered around the fire for a time of music-making, games and friendly chat. But the high point of this party came when one of the students, knowing that the

1

Director had many contacts abroad thanks to his ecumenical activities, asked if as a birthday present for him the seminary could make a visit to Sweden. The Lutheran Church of Sweden was taking a big interest in the Church Struggle going on in Germany and the idea was greeted with acclamation, strongly supported by the Director himself. The visit, lasting ten days, took place just a few weeks later in March.

This birthday incident and its aftermath might seem rather trivial in the total context of Dietrich Bonhoeffer's career, which combined profound theological and ethical thinking, costly engagement in the church's witness in the Nazi state, and eventual involvement in the political conspiracy against Hitler, which led to his execution at Flossenbürg execution camp in April 1945, just before the war in Europe ended. There are, however, two features of this story which point up essential features of how Bonhoeffer saw 'church', running counter to certain strongly held notions of the time in Germany. First, the very informality of that birthday-party and other like occasions at Finkenwalde signalled a rather unusual view of community in academic and clerical circles for that time. Dietrich Bonhoeffer was indeed officially designated 'Director' of the seminary, entitled to be addressed as 'Herr Direktor'. But from the outset he insisted that on a par with all the students he be styled *Bruder Bonhoeffer*—'Brother Bonhoeffer'. Life at Finkenwalde really would be life together: not hierarchical, but mutual. Second, for five years and more Bonhoeffer had been deeply involved in the international peace movement of the churches. He passionately believed that the church of Jesus Christ was inherently transnational, a single fellowship transcending all national boundaries and loyalties, a sign and instrument of God's command of peace to all peoples. In backing and leading the seminary's visit to Denmark and Sweden he knew what he was doing. He was 'cocking a snook' at the nationalism of the official Reich church which wanted to control all such contacts itself. The Reich church regarded international ecumenism as un-German, dangerous to German interests. When the Foreign Ministry of the Reich church found out about the visit there was were fury, especially as Bonhoeffer had secured an official invitation for it from the Swedish archbishop, Erling Eidem. Bonhoeffer was landed in deep trouble, incurring warnings that his influence 'was not conducive to German interests'[1] and that he was liable to the

---

1. See E Bethge, *Dietrich Bonhoeffer. A Biography,* revised and edited by Victoria J Barnett (Minneapolis: Fortress Press, 2000), 510.

accusation of being 'a pacifist and an enemy of the state'.[2] He may well have taken these as compliments.

Finkenwalde and its underlying theology in context

Bonhoeffer's seminary was already arousing suspicions even in some Confessing Church circles. It was rumoured that life at Finkenwalde resembled a Catholic monastery rather than a Lutheran preachers' seminary: as well as rigorous lectures in theology and classes in pastoralia, there was a disciplined daily life of communal prayer and private meditation; and even, it was said, private confession of sins one to another. So what had led this brilliant young theologian to take charge of what was at first sight a most un-Lutheran experiment in training future pastors? In a nutshell, Bonhoeffer believed that German Protestants no longer had any real understanding of what 'church' was all about, no idea of church as a *community* of people. If you went to church it was a basically individual affair of going to Sunday worship for your personal weekly dose of spiritual uplift, with no sense of being brought into active relationship with the others who were involved. Indeed, many thought that such individualism was the hallmark of good Protestantism as against Catholicism. This individualism proved fatally weak in face of Hitler's advent to power in 1933. But while Bonhoeffer from the start was deeply committed to the Confessing Church, he believed that resistance to the dark spell of Nazism required more than the finest theology or even the magnificent confession of faith set out in the famous Barmen Theological Declaration of 1934. It needed a renewal of community at the heart of the church's life, to counter the appeal of the fake community of racism and militarism, and to stiffen the resolve of those being tempted to retreat even further into an individualist, escapist piety. For that, the church needed adequately trained clergy, and an essential part of their formation would be the experience of living together, in shared learning and spiritual discipline. It needed, he dared to say, a new monasticism, not like the old but adequate to the present challenges. The Finkenwalde experiment lasted two years, during which time some 110 students passed through, until the seminary was closed

---

2. Bethge, *Dietrich Bonhoeffer*, 512.

down by the Gestapo in 1937. But, in a dispersed and even more clandestine way, the work continued for three more years.

Underlying all that Bonhoeffer was writing and teaching at Finkenwalde was not just a concern to meet the immediate needs of the hour in the Church Struggle, but a very definite theology of Christ and the church. He had worked this out long before the Nazi takeover and the onset of the Church Struggle. Indeed, it hails from his doctoral thesis which he completed in 1927 at the outrageously young age of 21. The subject of his thesis was the church, and its title was the Latin *Sanctorum Communio* (The Communion of Saints).[3] In his phrase, the church (that is the community or congregation which listens to God's word) is *Christ existing as community*. God in Christ becomes knowable in the community of his people. Revelation lands here on earth in a flesh and blood community, Christ existing as church-community. In saying this he claims that the church community is not a 'religious association', a kind of society or club of people with a like-minded religious interest. It is actually the body of Christ, as Paul states, its members sharing in the life of Christ and therefore members of one another. It's not a religious society; it's nothing less than the new humanity, God's new creation in Christ: a very 'high' view of the church.

Stellvertretung: 'vicarious representative action'

At this point, we must acquaint ourselves with a German word which, onwards from this early stage, runs like a stream through all Bonhoeffer's thinking, right to his last days in prison. It is a word which in *Sanctorum Communio* describes how Christ founds the church as his body, and constitutes how its members relate to one another. The word is *Stellvertretung*. Earlier English editions of Bonhoeffer translated it as 'deputyship'. In fact, it is not easy to find a completely satisfactory English equivalent. The new Bonhoeffer English Works Series offers 'vicarious representative action', action which is not just 'deputising' for someone in the familiar sense of, say, attending a meeting when they themselves are unable to attend, but of actually taking that person's place to the point of taking on his or her suffering, representing that person in their need before others, and speaking on his or

---

3.   Published as *DBWE* 1.

her behalf. (In not very serious vein, I recall a somewhat scurrilous instance of a plea for *Stellvertretung* during my first visit to Australia thirteen years ago. My wife and I were in a café in Apollo Bay, when a man walked in and quite publicly addressed his friends with a request: he had just received notice of a fine and penalty points from the Melbourne police for going through a red light a few days before. Would someone be willing to say that they had been driving his car that day, and collect the points on his behalf? I don't think he found any takers. They obviously don't believe in that form of *Stellvertretung* in Apollo Bay.)

For Bonhoeffer, *Stellvertretung* is most fully exemplified by Jesus Christ himself who did take our place as sinners on the cross, and who always exists as the love shown in that *Stellvertretung*. Equally it defines how members of the body of Christ are called and enabled to relate to one another, to be Christ to one another as Luther said, a forgiven and forgiving people. Bonhoeffer takes the traditional evangelical gospel and transmutes it into entirely relational terms. He moved on from *Sanctorum Communio*, but *Stellvertretung* remained a key concept for him, marking the trajectory of his life and thought, in a stream that acquired widening and deepening significance as it flowed onwards. The church is founded by, and lives by, *Stellvertretung* in its life together as a community of ministry.

Two books from Finkenwalde: *Discipleship* and *Life Together*

Two of Bonhoeffer's best-known and best-loved books were written out of his time at Finkenwalde. *Discipleship*[4] (still perhaps known to many under the title given to its first English translation, *The Cost of Discipleship*) is based mainly on his seminary lectures on the gospel accounts of the calling of the first disciples and the Sermon on the Mount, and on the Apostle Paul's teaching on the church as the body of Christ. Some of Bonhoeffer's most memorable phrases are found here: 'Cheap grace is the mortal enemy of our church. Our struggle today is for costly grace.'[5] 'Whenever Christ calls us, his call leads

---

4. *DBWE* 4.
5. Bonhoeffer, *DBWE* 4, 43.

us to death.'[6] Bonhoeffer relentlessly etches Christian life as pursuing the narrow way of a relationship focussed exclusively on Jesus Christ himself, come what may. In the context of the time when so many were tempted to follow the broad way, the populist way, of easy conformity to the world and the powers that be, shouting *Sieg Heil!*, its significance is clear. *Life Together*[7] is a much shorter book but no less challenging, and it is not surprising that the Finkenwalde experiment continues to inspire further ventures and thinking on Christian community.[8]

Surprises meet us at almost every page-turn in *Life Together*. If we expect eulogies on the wonder and beauty of Christian fellowship we are in for a rude shock. Indeed, several times Bonhoeffer warns us *off* forming or joining a community, especially if we have idealistic notions about it. The sooner we are disillusioned the better, he says, for community in Christ—whether in a seminary, a congregation or household or whatever—is not based on our visions however pious or romantic as to what it should be, but on the uncomfortable reality of its members as all-too-human people living by the forgiveness of sins. Here he puts flesh on *Stellvertretung*. Part of that life together, he says, is that of service, ministry to one another. He is very practical:

> [Thus] it is a good idea that all members receive a definite task to perform for the community, so that they may know in times of doubt that they too are not useless and incapable of doing anything. Every Christian community must know that not only do the weak need the strong, but also that the strong cannot exist without the weak. The elimination of the weak is the death of the community.[9]

In the sinister context of the Nazi programmes to eliminate mental and physical 'defectives', the resonances of the last sentence in this citation are clear. As so often, what Bonhoeffer says about the church

---

6. Bonhoeffer, *DBWE* 4, 87. The earlier translation (in *Cost of |Discipleship*) ran 'When Christ calls a man, he bids him come and die.'
7. Bonhoeffer, *DBWE* 5.
8. I commend the study by Craig Gardiner of the South Wales Baptist College in the UK, of Bonhoeffer's thought on community and the Iona Community in Scotland, founded by George Macleod, *Melodies of a New Monasticism* (Eugene, Oregon: Cascade Books, 2018).
9. Bonhoeffer, *DBWE* 5, 96.

is not *just* about the church. For him the church as community in Christ is called to exhibit God's new creation of *humanity* as a whole. How members of the body of Christ relate to one another will typically be counter-cultural, especially where the prevailing culture is one of authoritarian, hectoring demands for obedience. Pastors, for instance, notes Bonhoeffer, assume that everyone wants to hear them speak, but the first service one owes to others in the community is that of *listening*: 'We should listen with the ears of God, so that we can speak the Word of God.'[10] Then there is the ministry of active helpfulness, even in minor external matters. 'Nobody is too good for the lowest service.'[11] Third, and most important, there is the service of *bearing with others*, in accordance with Paul's injunction, 'Bear one another's burdens, and in this way, you will fulfil the law of Christ' (Galatians 6:2). Forbearance with others' sins means the burden of suffering. 'The burden of human beings was even for God so heavy that God had to go to the cross suffering under it.'[12] Hence, too, the service of hearing another's confession and, in all humility, of speaking and hearing the Word of God one with another. This view of community goes much further than conventional superficialities about 'fellowship'. Bonhoeffer's views on ministry, as I have already indicated, are in marked contrast to the Nazified ethos of *Führerprinzip*, leadership based solely on power and sheer assertion of authority and the dubious adulation of mass popularity. Pastors are not called to cajole or manipulate people, or force them into their own mould, but to let Christ be formed in the community. We find no expositions of 'management' techniques in the church, and all the accompanying jargon of secular corporate life and decision-making which some church circles are tempted to adopt (at the same time, ironically, as they are being questioned in corporate business life). Still less does Bonhoeffer give houseroom to personality cults and the worst excesses of the celebrity culture: 'The community of faith does not need brilliant personalities but faithful servants of Jesus Christ and of one another. It does not lack the former but the latter.'[13]

Indeed, we find in Bonhoeffer a repeated emphasis on a *shared* ministry. In his classes at Finkenwalde he has some very interesting

---

10. Bonhoeffer, *DBWE* 5, 99.
11. Bonhoeffer, *DBWE* 5, 99.
12. Bonhoeffer, *DBWE* 5, 100.
13. Bonhoeffer, *DBWE* 5, 107.

things to say about preaching, for example, including remarks under the heading, 'The How of evangelisation' as a shared enterprise. 'The bringer of [God's word] should be not an individual but a church-community, that is, several people as a small church-community, as a brotherhood living together under the word . . . [E]arly Christian proclamation, even that of Paul, who was called alone, was not solitary . . . To what extent does that also apply to the pastoral office, namely, that the one-man system actually represents an accommodation to secular vocations?'[14] This 'core-group' should be a community of prayer with the pastor. It is thus a shared ministry. We hear some striking admonitions, for example, 'Being completely exhausted after a sermon is a bad sign; it derives from an improper disposition. It is not the pastor who is to deplete himself in the pulpit but rather God.'[15]

What about the world?

Bonhoeffer's time at Finkenwalde and shortly afterwards might seem indeed to have been a monastic phase of his life, insulated from the world outside, and people sometimes contrast what he wrote in *Discipleship* and *Life Together* with what he went on to write in his wartime *Ethics* and above all in his prison letters, about faith's responsibility in the world and the 'worldliness' of Christianity. But I do not believe there were any sudden breaks in the course of Bonhoeffer's thinking—sharp turns yes, but with definite continuities. Bonhoeffer concludes *Discipleship* by summarising the whole of the scriptural witness to God's purpose with humankind as the creation of the image of Christ, the restoration of the divine image, in us. Our goal as human beings is to be shaped into the form of the incarnate, crucified and transfigured Christ. Then comes this remarkable passage, one of the most remarkable Bonhoeffer ever wrote, and crucial for understanding the way his mind was moving, just as life was becoming more difficult for him under the increasingly oppressive grip of the regime:

> Christ has taken on this *human form*. He became a human being like us. In his humanity and lowliness we recognize our own form. He became like human beings, so that we would

---

14. Bonhoeffer, *DBWE* 14, 521.
15. Bonhoeffer, *DBWE* 14, 530.

be like him. In Christ's incarnation all of humanity regains the dignity of bearing the image of God. Whoever from now on attacks the least of the people attacks Christ, who took on human form and who in himself has restored the image of God for all who bear a human countenance. In community with the incarnate one, we are once again given our true humanity. With it, we are delivered from the isolation caused by sin, and at the same time restored to the whole of humanity. Inasmuch as we participate in Christ, the incarnate one, we also have a part in all of humanity, which is borne by him. Since we know ourselves to be accepted and borne within the humanity of Jesus, our new humanity now also consists in bearing the troubles and sins of all others. The incarnate one transforms his disciples into brothers and sisters of all human beings. The 'philanthropy' of God (Titus 3:4) that became evident in the incarnation of Christ is the reason for Christians to love every human being on earth as a brother or sister. The form of the incarnate one transforms the church-community into the body of Christ upon which all of humanity's sin and trouble fall, and by which alone these troubles and sins are borne.[16]

Notice the language of 'bearing' in this passage. This is about ministry as *Stellvertretung* at a new level. Reading that passage, one feels as if the whole of *Discipleship* has been leading us along a very narrow defile, focussed entirely on the way of Christ, Christ and his way alone, Christ leading us to the cross. Then all of a sudden, this narrow defile on which we have been walking opens out onto a panorama of the whole world. The Christ whom we have been following to the exclusion of all others, turns out to be the one who identifies himself with all people in their suffering and need, and so our faith likewise is called to embrace all humanity without barriers; thereby we allow the image of God to be recreated in us. So Bonhoeffer here is taking up his early notion of the church being Christ-existing-as-community and now placing it in the wider context of that church being Christ-existing-as-community in *Stellvertretung* for the whole world. He himself had in effect already pointed this out four years earlier in 1933, during the early persecutions of the Jews, in his paper 'The Church and the Jewish Question'. He stated, 'The church has an unconditional obligation toward the victims of any societal order,

---

16. Bonhoeffer, *DBWE* 4, 285.

even if they do not belong to the Christian community'.[17] That precept is now grounded in his incarnational doctrine of Christ and human community, in which *Stellvertretung* is central. Bonhoeffer's notion of our communion with Christ restoring in us the image of God (an understanding which owes much to the second century church father Irenaeus) also assumes a notion of salvation somewhat at odds with certain brands of evangelical preaching. Bonhoeffer always affirmed that 'Christ died for our sins', but not in a way that portrays Christ as paying a price external to us, a salvation to which we relate by accepting a bargain which merely 'imputes' to us a righteousness we do not really have. Rather, for Bonhoeffer we are actually drawn into Christ's righteousness in communion with him, and thereby also into his solidarity with all humanity. The implications for our understanding of 'mission' and 'evangelisation' are immense, not least their costliness.

Into dark places

This understanding of Jesus Christ as the supreme embodiment of *Stellvertretung* is what accompanied Bonhoeffer into the following tumultuous years of the war, during which he entered into the political conspiracy against Hitler. Now he devoted his writing time to his *Ethics*, which is much occupied with the question of what it means to act responsibly in society. Reading between the lines of the *Ethics* we can see how the context of resistance and conspiracy was pressing upon his mind. All the complexities and ambiguities of involvement in a plot which would eventually require an attempt at assassination of the head of state, and the outcome of which could not be wholly foreseen, brought him face to face with the question of guilt, and of whether in such a situation of massive politicised evil manifest on the scale of the Holocaust, one could ever be guilt-free. Bonhoeffer's guiding light here is again Jesus as the supreme embodiment of vicarious representative action. Jesus, he says, is not 'the individual who seeks to attain his own ethical perfection. Instead, he lives only as the one who in himself has taken on and bears the selves of all human beings'

---

17. Bonhoeffer, *DBWE* 12, 365. It is in this paper that Bonhoeffer made his remark that eventually the church may have to consider 'putting a spoke' in the wheel rather than just bandaging up the victims.

including their guilt.[18] Jesus does not come teaching love as the ethical ideal; he actually loves real human beings. Such love cannot be regulated by any law. 'Jesus does not want to be considered the only perfect one, to look down on a humanity perishing under its guilt . . . Love for real human beings leads into the solidarity of human guilt.'[19] Responsible action, if it is motivated by love for real people, as was Jesus, will lead to solidarity with their guilt and indeed will be prepared to become guilty for their sake, rather than preserve one's own supposed innocence. This is *Stellvertretung* at its most profound. It accompanied Bonhoeffer the conspirator into some very dark places. Bonhoeffer's great friend and biographer, Eberhard Bethge once told me of one winter's evening early in the war, when he and Bonhoeffer were staying in the country home of Bonhoeffer's brother in law Hans von Dohnanyi, who was one of the master minds on the civilian wing of the conspiracy. The three of them were talking by the fireside, and Dohnanyi asked Dietrich, 'What about the saying of Jesus, "Whoever takes the sword will perish by the sword." Does that mean us? We are taking up the sword.' Dietrich answered, 'Yes, that's true. That word is still valid for us now. The time needs exactly those people who do that, and let Jesus' saying be true. We take the sword and are prepared to perish by it. Taking up guilt means accepting the consequences of it. Maybe God will save us but'—a long pause—'first of all you must be prepared to accept the consequences.'[20] That was indeed a dark place to be in, but as well as illuminating that extreme situation, Bonhoeffer also uses *Stellvertretung* as a lens to view how all true human social relationships, whether in the family, or the world of work, or education or whatever, in some way manifest elements of vicarious representative action, the kind of action consummated by Christ.[21] That is a sign of the lordship of Christ over all things and all people.

---

18. Bonhoeffer, *DBWE* 6, 231.
19. Bonhoeffer, *DBWE* 6, 233.
20. K Clements, *What Freedom? The Persistent Challenge of Dietrich Bonhoeffer* (Bristol: Bristol Baptist College, 1990), 37.
21. *Cf* also in Australia, Victoria's own experiences of the instinctive, spontaneous outpourings of communal solidarity in the wake of the 'Black Saturday' bush fires of 2009, and in February 2019 the public vigils for the murdered Arab-Israeli student Aiia Maasarwe in Melbourne.

In a world without religion?

Stellvertretung therefore marks the trajectory which Bonhoeffer's thinking, and indeed so much of his activity, took onwards from his first years as a theologian. But what about his latest phase, from his imprisonment in April 1943 to his execution at Flossenbürg concentration camp two years later? Did *Stellvertretung* really survive that time during which, especially from end April 1944, he penned to Eberhard Bethge those startling letters[22] exploring what a 'religionless Christianity' in a 'world come of age' might look like, a world in which we have to live 'as if God was not there'. In those letters, Bonhoeffer described what he saw as a long historical process now coming to completion, of the end of 'religion'. By 'religion' he means, quite specifically, thinking which is 'metaphysical' confining God to a realm outside this visible world of time and space; thinking which is individualistic, concerned with *my* salvation; and thinking which sees that salvation only in a realm the other side of death. What survives as 'religion' today is in Bonhoeffer's mind always something partial, a sacred sector of life, whereas it is our life as a whole which is claimed and transformed by God: 'Jesus calls not to a new religion but to life.'[23] Religion means thinking of God as a being who is outside and beyond our life in this world, and who is only called in from outside when our human powers fall short. That God of religion is fading away from human life today. But in any case, such a God has very little to do with the one the Bible calls God, whose kingdom is the transformation of this world into a community with God in righteousness and peace.

There has been huge discussion, continuing still today from our vantage point nearly seventy-five years after his death, on whether Bonhoeffer got it wrong. After all, religion in some shape or form, good or bad, is very much alive in our world today. But he was surely right in perceiving that a major shift was under way, in the Western world at any rate, in relation to traditional religion and expressions of faith. Faith is no longer the assumed default position in the societies you and I live in—you only have to read our daily newspapers (even, or perhaps especially, *The Age*[24]) to be struck by how far daily and

---

22. Bonhoeffer, *DBWE* 8.
23. Bonhoeffer, *DBWE* 8, 482.
24. A Melbourne daily newspaper.

public affairs are pursued without any reference to God, church or religion of any sort. The American philosopher and historian, Charles Taylor, was surely right in seeing that a sea-change in Western culture became evident in the 1960s. It was not so much a new philosophy that came about, but a new way in which people felt and perceived themselves to be in relation to the big dimensions of life: 'That each one of us has his/her own way of realising our humanity, that it is important to find and live out one's own, as against surrendering to conformity with a model imposed on us from outside, or the previous generation, or religious or political authority.'[25] This might seem to be sanctioning the very kind of individualism that Bonhoeffer and others warn against, but that is not necessarily so. A communal form of faith is still very much a *sine qua non* of Christianity today, but it is an *option*, to be embraced in freedom. It cannot be assumed, nor imposed from above. In that sense, we are in a post-Christian world, or perhaps better a post-Christendom world, a world no longer under assumed Christian institutional dominance, and in a culture no longer of unquestioned Christian values. In fact, Taylor's insight resonates with the criticism that Bonhoeffer in his prison writings makes of his great mentor, Karl Barth who, Bonhoeffer says, now comes across as presenting people with a 'take it or leave it' attitude to Christianity as a fixed body of beliefs to be swallowed whole. But if the world is 'post-Christian', or post-Christendom, it is not post-*Christ*. Bonhoeffer is absolutely sure of that. This is the main thrust of these prison writings, which focus not just on what is happening to the world but how and where Christ is in it as a transformative presence with us, the place where God is rediscovered not as a remote being beyond this world, but the beyond in the midst, the truly transcendent one at the centre of life. As his fateful time in prison drew on, in August 1944 he wrote an 'Outline for a Book' which included these notes:

> Encounter with Jesus Christ. Experience that here is a reversal of all human existence, in the very fact that Jesus only 'is there for others'. Jesus's 'being-for-others' is the experience of transcendence! . . . Faith is participating in this being of

---

25. Charles Taylor, *A Secular Age* (Cambridge MA: Belknap, 2011), 475. See also the extensive discussion of Taylor in James Gerard McEvoy, *Leaving Christendom for Good. Church World Dialogue in a Secular Age* (Plymouth: Lexington Books, 2014).

> Jesus . . . Our relationship to God is a new life in 'being there for others', through participation in the being of Jesus. The transcendent is not the infinite, unattainable tasks, but the neighbour within reach in any given situation.[26]

This leads to the conclusion:

> The church is church only when it is there for others . . . The church must participate in the worldly tasks of life in the community–not dominating but helping and serving. It must tell people in every calling what a life with Christ is, what it means 'to be there for others'.[27]

This is Bonhoeffer's basic guideline for ministry today: to take part in the transformative life of Christ in the world. While the term *Stellvertretung* does not occur explicitly in those letters, its meaning comes to the full flower of significance for Bonhoeffer, and for us too if we are looking for his guidelines for ministry in the 'post-Christian world', where religion tends to flourish only as a tool for those who want to use it for their own purposes of power and prestige, divisively and destructively. For example, almost at the end of his long poem 'The Death of Moses', penned in September 1944 after the failure of the 20 July attempt on Hitler's life, and aware what his own fate was now likely to be, he writes:

> To punish sin, to forgive you are moved;
> O God, this people have I truly loved.
>
> That I bore its shame and sacrifices
> And saw its salvation—that suffices.[28]

That is *Stellvertretung*, life with others, life for others.

Transformation for maturity

The fundamental wisdom that Bonhoeffer sets out for ministry in our world is thus a ministry which serves the transformative growth

---

26. Bonhoeffer, *DBWE* 8, 501.
27. Bonhoeffer, *DBWE* 8, 503.
28. Bonhoeffer, *DBWE* 5, 240–241.

of people becoming not religious, but fully human after the manner of Jesus Christ, to be 'there for others'. It means nurturing church-communities of persons who grow, in the words of the Apostle Paul, 'to *maturity*, to the measure if the full stature of Christ' (Eph 4:13), that is, ready for all the responsibilities of *Stellvertretung*, life with and for others, with all its joys and risks, and especially in solidarity with those who suffer and are not reckoned to count in society. In 1939, at the start of the Second World War, one of Bonhoeffer's British friends in the ecumenical movement, the Scottish lay theologian and ecumenist, JH Oldham, launched his fortnightly *Christian Newsletter*. Throughout the war and after it was a means of information and sharing of views on how Christians and all concerned people could respond to face the dreadful realities of war and all the challenges it would bring for those concerned for the future social order. In the opening number of the *Newsletter* Oldham addressed the subject of fear: 'What holds us back more than anything else is fear—fear not only of death but of life.'[29] Mature life means making decisions, shouldering responsibilities and taking risks, and acting even when we cannot be sure of the outcome. It is the way of faith, hope and love. It is, in fact, *Stellvertretung*. It is a very worldly ministry, but does not conform to what either the powers that be or popular opinion expects or wants of religion. We can list certain points at which it challenges our personal and cultural mores, and our churchly assumptions too.

Stellvertretung connotes not an idea, but an action, an intensely loving action, divine and human. Bonhoeffer emphatically warns against pure verbalising of the gospel of Christ. Words alone, he warns, however theological religious or pious, no longer convey who Christ is today: 'the church's word gains weight and power not through concepts but by example.'[30] Many of us can testify to that, I am sure. I like to collect illustrations of the very point Bonhoeffer makes. One example from the UK is the BBC World Affairs Editor John Simpson, who has spent many years knocking around the world and covering some of the most terrible scenes of conflict (twenty years ago I met him in a Belgrade hotel breakfast bar during the NATO bombing of Belgrade). He tells how his own Christian faith, which he thought he had outgrown decades before, came alive again in South Africa, through wit-

29. JH Oldham, *Christian News-Letter,* No 0 (18 October 1939).
30. Bonhoeffer, *DBWE* 8, 504.

nessing at first hand the ending of apartheid and especially the role of people like Desmond Tutu as agents of reconciliation. Contradicting the current cultural assumption that life is about protecting yourself from whatever discomforts us, he writes in his memoir:

> But what if . . . the point of living isn't to be placid and happy and untouched by the world, but to be deeply, painfully sensitive to it, to see its cruelty and savagery for what they are, and accept all this as readily as we accept its beauty? To be touched by it, loved by it, hurt by it even, but not to be indifferent to it?[31]

That's a rather good expression of 'religionless Christianity'; or rather 'Christ-full life in the world'.

Stellvertretung involves a spirituality of movement. An essential part of life together as taught by Bonhoeffer at Finkenwalde, and of life for others as he practised it in prison, is intercessory prayer. Intercession is apt to become a cheap matter of simply ticking off the known needs of individuals or communities or nations, job done. The verb 'to intercede' derives from two Latin words, *inter* (between) and *cedere* (to move). In intercessory prayer we don't just 'remember' or 'think about' certain people or situations: we *move ourselves* in spirit (and then, if possible, in body) to where they are, ponder what they are going through, try to identify with it, and then *move* again to God and face God with what we have taken upon ourselves. There is no more profound example of intercessory prayer than the long poem Bonhoeffer wrote in Tegel prison, 'Night Voices',[32] where he makes his own what he imagines his fellow-prisoners—not political prisoners like himself but mostly solders who have fallen foul of military law—are muttering in their uneasy sleep, sinners and sinned against, anxious, guilty and fearful of what awaits them.

The way of *Stellvertretung* runs counter to every form of self-enclosed life which regards any claim of what is outside of us as intrusive and a violation of our personal freedom, a threat to our well-being. *Stellvertretung* challenges the self-drawn boundaries of communal identity that claim quasi-sacred significance. The supreme

---

31. John Simpson, *Not Quite World's End: A Traveller's Tales* (London: Macmillan, 2007), 460–461.
32. Bonhoeffer, *DBWE* 8, 462–470.

exemplar of *Stellvertretung*, Jesus Christ, took the place of all people before God, and represented God to all people, the Jew and the gentile alike, even to the cross. *Stellvertretung*, vicarious representative action, challenges all our tendencies to erect self-made barriers round ourselves. What is responsible action cannot be determined or limited by the boundaries of race, class, nation, or gender. In our time, nationalism is rampant again, and moreover co-opting religion into its armoury, as in President Narendra Modi's India, Vladimir Putin's Russia, President Tayyip Erdogan's Turkey and Donald Trump's USA, and you yourselves may have comments to make on the Australian scene. What people glibly call patriotism is itself becoming a new religion. Bonhoeffer's theologically-based critique of all forms of nationalism during the 1930s, and his insistence that the ecumenical fellowship of Jesus Christ stands for a totally different order of human solidarity, needs to be revisited and claimed as an essential part of the church's ministry today. This belief never left Bonhoeffer. Among his last known words, the day before he was executed, is a message to his English friend Bishop George Bell: 'Tell him, that with him I believe in the reality of our international Christian fellowship which rises above all national interests and conflicts, and that our victory is certain.'[33] I should add that in Britain today, in the midst of our confusion over our relations with the rest of Europe, we as much as any other people are desperately in need of a mature vision of what it means to be part of the wider family of people. To adapt a famous English poem, no *nation* is an island, entire of itself, every nation is a piece of the continent, a part of the main.

Stellvertretung means calling government, and all power and authority, to account on behalf of those who, it is claimed, will benefit from policies for the common good. We shall identify with refugees and asylum seekers because at the table of our Lord, when we reach out for the bread and wine, we know ourselves to be refugees and asylum seekers yearning for grace and thankful for it. Vicarious representative action does not shrink from but seeks responsible use of the God-given resources of science, technology and all human wisdom. In our day, more than in Bonhoeffer's time, we are coming to recognise that this includes representation on behalf of the whole created order of the earth threatened by climate change and environmental

---

33. Bethge, *Dietrich Bonhoeffer*, 1022, n 54.

degradation. It means continually asking, are you aware of the consequences for others, of your decisions and actions? Who is likely to be hurt by your actions, or non-actions? It is a question both for pastors and congregations: What kind of Christ is it who we want to be existing as our communities? The fake Christ whom we want to bolster our differences and sense of importance, or the Christ who calls us to share his costly intercession for each and all? What kind of persons are we hoping to nurture through our worship and life together: persons who want to be safely marked out by their virtue, or those who are joyously thankful for grace and so dare to eat with tax collectors and sinners? What kind of impact upon society do we want to make? To restore the old Christendom where church and state went hand in glove, where institutional Christianity dominated everything, or do we want to seek embodiments of vicarious representative action wherever and by whomever they enhance justice and promote peace in the world? As disciples (not owners!) of Jesus Christ we shall affirm and uphold appearances of *Stellvertretung* wherever we encounter them in the world, and this is very pertinent to interfaith relations in the common search for human welfare.[34]

Still discovering: Christ in this world

We can describe our world in various ways: the post-religious world, the post-Christian world, the post-Christendom world, the post-colonial world. But it is still he world in which Christ comes to live fully and to bring life in its fullness, by his vicarious representative action, and calls us to be with him there. *Stellvertretung* remains, and will ever be, the way of Christ in the midst of the world, and our way of ministry with him, the way to the truly human fullness of life. John Matthews, Lutheran pastor and Bonhoeffer scholar in Minnesota, USA, sums up Bonhoeffer's guidelines for us better than any I know.

> In a world and church where pain and suffering are seen as God's curse or absence, the disciples of Jesus Christ are called to live in solidarity with those who suffer, in the knowledge that God suffers and calls people to share in God's suffering; in a world and church where fear of God and anxiety for

---

34. For an instance in the writer's own experience, see K Clements, *Look Back in Hope. An Ecumenical Life* (Eugene, Oregon: Resource Publications, 2017), 309–310.

the future cause people to assume a position of immature dependence before the Almighty, Jesus Christ calls disciples to trust the love of God and accept the role of stewarding the world in a mature and interdependent manner.[35]

The temptation is always for us to try and locate God in a different world from that which we are actually experiencing; rather like the Chinese emperor who, so the story goes, became so unpopular with his people that he eventually asked his advisers to find him another and more amenable people for him to rule over. Ministry means sticking with this world where we are now, even the post-Christian world, not the imagined world of yesterday nor the dreamt-of world of tomorrow, but this very same world where God often seems absent or forgotten, as the world where we find and serve Christ the *Stellvertreter*. One time when I was with Eberhard Bethge in his study I asked him where the original prison letters that he received from Bonhoeffer were now kept. 'Oh', he said, pointing to his desk, 'in here! Would you like to see any of them? Which one in particular?' Without hesitation I asked to see the one he wrote on 21 July 1944, the day after the failure of the plot against Hitler. A moment later it was in my hand. It felt almost like holding the original of one of Paul's epistles. It begins, *Heute*—'today', in other words *this* very fearful and fateful day—and then goes on with his marvellous statement of faith, in which he reviews his life, now surely with its end in sight, and what he has learnt on the way:

> I discovered, and am still discovering to this day, that one only learns to have faith by living in the full this-worldliness of life . . . living fully in the midst of life's tasks, successes and failures, experiences, and perplexities then one takes seriously not one's own sufferings but rather the sufferings of God in the world. Then one stands awake with Christ in Gethsemane . . . And this is how one becomes a human being, a Christian. How should one become arrogant over successes or shaken by one's failures when one shares in God's suffering in the life of the world?[36]

---

35. John Matthews, *Anxious Souls Will Ask: The Christ-Centered Spirituality of Dietrich Bonhoeffer* (Grand Rapids, Michigan: Eerdmans, 2005), 67.
36. Bonhoeffer, *DBWE* 8, 486.

Conclusion

'I discovered, and am still discovering to this day . . .' I wonder, when he was writing these lines, did his mind go back to that birthday party at Finkenwalde eight years earlier? That birthday party was one significant point on his journey of discovery. We, too, are all invited to make that journey from where we are now. It is a journey to which we are called by Christ: not to religion but to life in all its dimensions, life with others, life for others. The post-Christian world is still Christ's world, and must be lived in, in Christ's way. That is Bonhoeffer's basic wisdom for ministry today.

Vol 6 No 1/2018

Earthly Christianity: Bonhoeffer's Contribution to Ecotheology and Ecoethics

Dianne Rayson

Introduction

Bonhoeffer's 'unfinished symphony' of theology is rich for exploration, creative extension, and application. Accordingly, this paper considers Bonhoeffer's notion of 'worldly Christianity' (his theorising of what Christianity might be in the post war age) in the context of the new age, the Anthropocene (the present geological epoch determined by human intervention). It describes how Bonhoeffer's christological theology might contribute to contemporary ecotheological and ecoethical concerns. Bonhoeffer's worldly Christianity becomes, in this age, more appropriately described as 'Earthly Christianity' and humans as *Homo cosmicos*—both belonging to the world and being a responsible citizen of it. Relational 'Earthly Christianity' drives an ecoethic of responsibility and sacrifice that recognises the new context—two components of ethics that Bonhoeffer articulated as *Stellvertretung* and *Sachgemäßheit*.

The problem of the *Anthropocene*

This is the *Anthropocene*: the age of humans, when the world has not only 'come of age' (*Mündigkeit*)[1] but entered a new age of unprecedented existential uncertainty. Human behaviour has disrupted Earth's homeostatic systems and feedback mechanisms in ways previously unknown to the planet. The new epoch is characterised by the instability of climate change and its corollary, 'weather weirding', two of the symptoms of global warming, whilst other parameters,

---

1. Bonhoeffer, *DBWE* 8, 450–51, 457, 482.

described as 'planetary boundaries' are also being breached.[2] Perhaps the most significant of these is the loss of biodiversity closely linked to land use changes and resulting in Earth's sixth mass extinction event. This, in turn, threatens our own viability on Earth.

The great acceleration describes the logarithmic rise in population growth, affluence, and the use of technology since 1950.[3] Together these have driven excessive consumption and pollution that accentuated the large scale burning of fossil fuels characteristic of human development since the Industrial Revolution. There is clear evidence for fundamental shifts in the state and functioning of the earth system as a result.[4] These are beyond the range of variability that humans have ever experienced and create a precarious non-analogue state. Earth has moved out of the relatively stable state of the Holocene—the past 11,500 years in which humans have flourished and civilisations developed. The victims are quickly becoming apparent; the world's poor, who have been the least culpable, are the first and greatest sufferers of sea level rise, food and water insecurity, and civil unrest,[5] and political and social structures, including religious ones, are yet to respond adequately to the new ethical demands of this age. The ethical concerns are not only human: they relate to our fellow species and natural features as we corrupt the entire biosphere.

Bonhoeffer's contribution

Precisely because anthropogenic climate change is a symptom of human beliefs, attitudes, and behaviours means that it is a topic for theological reflection both in terms of better articulating a theological understanding of our relationship to Earth and her creatures, and to frame an ethical response to the problem. Clifford Green has

---

2. Johan Rockström *et al*, 'A Safe Operating Space for Humanity', in *Nature* 461/7263 (24 Sept 2009): 472–75.

3. Will Steffen *et al*, 'The Trajectory of the Anthropocene: The Great Acceleration', in *The Anthropocene Review*, 2/1 (2015): 81–98.

4. Gerardo Ceballos *et al*, 'Accelerated Modern Human–Induced Species Losses: Entering the Sixth Mass Extinction', in *Science Advances* 1/5 (2015): e1400253; Chris D Thomas *et al*, 'Extinction Risk from Climate Change', in *Nature* 427/6970 (2004): 145–48.

5. Camilo Mora *et al*, 'The Projected Timing of Climate Departure from Recent Variability', in *Nature* 502 (2013): 183–87.

proposed that Bonhoeffer's creative theology represents a paradigm shift for theology in the twenty-first century, characterised not only by Christ being *pro Me*, but also *pro Mundo*, for the world.[6] I suggest that, in support of Green's notion, Bonhoeffer's prison speculation of 'worldly Christianity',[7] with christological roots going back to his earliest works, can be further interpreted to have an even more profound application in the Anthropocene, namely, that of 'Earthly Christianity'. The potential for reading Bonhoeffer with attention to his contribution to ecotheology and ecoethics has been identified by Larry Rasmussen[8] and others, and this paper represents a response to Rasmussen's call to systematically develop Bonhoeffer's writings the seminal moral issue not only of our time, but that humanity has ever faced.[9] As David Attenborough expressed at the 2018 UN Climate Change Summit in Poland, 'the continuation of our civilisations and the natural world on which we depend' is at stake.[10] Theology is a necessary discourse partner if the issue is to be understood and the necessary action taken.

I suggest here several elements of Bonhoeffer's theological contribution. The first is Bonhoeffer's notion of sociality that derives from his articulation of Christology, and the ecological parallels to such sociality; and the second is the ecoethics that can be derived from his works. Together these can inform a fresh interpretation of Bonhoeffer's 'worldly Christianity' as 'Earthly Christianity'. Rather than identifying a specific Bonhoefferian 'ecotheology', Bonhoeffer's thinking

---

6. Clifford J Green, '*Christus in Mundo, Christus pro Mundo*: Bonhoeffer's Foundations for a New Christian Paradigm', in *Bonhoeffer, Religion and Politics. Fourth International Bonhoeffer Colloquium*, edited by Christiane Tietz and Jens Zimmerman, International Bonhoeffer Interpretations (IBI) 4 (Frankfurt am Main: Peter Lang, 2012), 11–36.

7. Bonhoeffer, *DBWE* 8, 364.

8. Larry L Rasmussen, 'Bonhoeffer: Ecological Theologian', in *Bonhoeffer and Interpretive Theory: Essays on Methods and Understanding. International Bonhoeffer Interpretations (IBI)* sixth edition. Peter Frick (Frankfurt am Maim: Peter Lang, 2014), 251–68; 'Bonhoeffer and the Anthropocene', in *Stellenbosch Theological Journal* 55, No Supp 1 (2015): 941–54.

9. Peter Singer, 'Climate Change: Our Greatest Ethical Challenge', (lecture, University of Chicago, 23 October 2015). See also, Kevin Rudd, 'Climate Change the Great Moral Challenge of Our Generation', (Canberra: LaborTV, 2007).

10. David Attenborough, 'The People's Seat', (speech to COP24, Katowice, Poland: United Nations, 2018).

provides the tools to authentically engage with the theological and ethical demands of the age.

Bonhoeffer's concern with the natural world is demonstrably deeper than a culturally informed appreciation of the outdoors, although there is ample evidence of this. The Christology lectures were prepared in the woods, whilst he sojourned in his family holiday house. In prison he yearns for the sunshine:

> I should really like to feel the full force of it again, burning on one's skin and gradually making one's whole body glow, so that one knows again that one is a corporeal being. I'd like to get tired by the sun instead of by books and thinking. I'd like to have it awaken my animal existence . . . I'd like, just for once, not just to see the sun and sip at it a little, but to experience it bodily.[11]

In that letter from 30 June 1944 Bonhoeffer speculates on the effect that the sun has on creativity and imagination, and whether this influences our desire for hot countries. Bonhoeffer's biography exemplifies the flourishing life in body and mind, just as science itself shows the diminishing division between the two. This validation of the material, including the human body, derives from Bonhoeffer's Christology and informs what we might now portray as pre-emptive ecotheological thinking.

In any case, Bonhoeffer provides an indication of what science is increasingly affirming: that humans are not actors performing 'within' an environment that serves as our theatre. We are embedded within an interrelated ecology and as much as we desire to manipulate it, we are instead influenced by it, even to our very core. Our mood and cognition, at least to some extent, are shaped: by our interactions with other microbial species, and the effects of sunlight, colours, and ions.[12]

---

11. Bonhoeffer, *DBWE* 8, 448–49.
12. Jeffrey M Craig, Alan C Logan, and Susan L Prescott, 'Natural Environments, Nature Relatedness and the Ecological Theater: Connecting Satellites and Sequencing to Shinrin-Yoku', in *Journal of Physiological Anthropology* 35/1 (2016): DOI 10.1186/s40101-016-0083-9; Patrick ten Brink *et al*, *The Health and Social Benefits of Nature and Biodiversity Protection: A Report for the European Commission* (London/Brussels: Institute for European Environmental Policy, 2016).

In his farewell sermon to the Barcelona congregation, Bonhoeffer draws together the human biophilic disposition with the problem of domination, or what he would later articulate as the 'attempted mastery of nature':[13]

> Whoever has felt but once how nature can embrace us and rob us of our senses, perhaps at a quiet forest lake in the evening, a lake that shines into our soul like the deep eyes of a child, perhaps before the simplicity of a beautiful forest flower we encounter like a pure greeting nature sends to its children; whoever has felt but once how creation, how Mother Earth seizes the heart—that person will know forever what he or she lacks . . . [A] rift runs through the world, a rift that is visible in nature where human beings are, and that disappears where human beings are no more.[14]

The relationship between humans and Earth is conflicted and yet best understood Christologically.

Bonhoeffer's Christology for Earth

The Christology lectures of 1932 frame Christ as incarnate, crucified, and risen, summarised in *Ethics*:

> In the becoming human we recognize God's love toward God's creation, in the crucifixion God's judgment on all flesh, and in the resurrection God's purpose for a new world.[15]

That God would become flesh in the world—*Christus in Mundo*—honours the fleshly form of all creatures such that 'all humanity regains the dignity of bearing the image of God'.[16] Christ present in history establishes the ongoing presence of Christ in Word, sacrament and in

---

13. Bonhoeffer, *DBWE* 11, 246. See Dianne Rayson, 'Bonhoeffer and "the Right to Self-Assertion": Understanding Theologically the Mastery of Nature and War', in *Ecological Aspects of War: Religious Perspectives from Australia*, A Forum for Theology in the World, edited Anne F Elvey *et al* (Adelaide: ATF Press, 2016), 95–110.
14. Bonhoeffer, *DBWE* 10, 546.
15. Bonhoeffer, *DBWE* 6, 157.
16. Bonhoeffer, *DBWE* 4, 285.

the church-community. However, it is Bonhoeffer's attention to the revelation of God in history upon which the validation of the material world depends. The act of the incarnation demonstrates God's intentional posture of being *pro Me*, making reconciliation with God an 'ontological reality'.[17] The human brokenness and division from God represented by Adam is restored and made whole in Christ who comes to the world as the vulnerable one who is broken. Eva Harasta has proposed that Bonhoeffer's identification of Christ with Adam, at once guilty and redeemed, could best be described as 'Adam in Christ',[18] a notion that both interprets Bonhoeffer's soteriology, and reinforces the inseparability of earthly things with the spiritual. Furthermore, God's reconciliation through Christ is unlimited: Bonhoeffer states, 'Nothing is lost; in Christ all things are taken up, preserved, albeit in transfigured form, transparent, clear, liberated from the torment of self-serving demands . . . [not] distorted by sin'.[19] Indeed, reality does not exist outside Christ, who is the centre of a unified, restored reality, 'the one realm of the Christ-reality'[*Christuswirklichkeit*].[20] In Bonhoeffer's words,

> In the body of Jesus Christ, God is united with humankind, all humanity is accepted by God, and the world is reconciled to God. There is no part of the world, no matter how lost, no matter how godless, that has not been accepted by God in Jesus Christ and reconciled to God . . . The world belongs to Christ . . .[21]

Furthermore, 'In the body of Jesus Christ humanity is now truly and bodily accepted; it is accepted as it is, out of God's mercy'.[22] In these passages, Bonhoeffer expresses God's universal soteriological intention, namely, that all humanity, and indeed the world, is reconciled.

---

17. Clifford J Green, 'Editor's Introduction DBWE 6' (Minneapolis: Fortress, 2005), 6.
18. Eva Harasta, 'Christ Becoming Pluralist: Bonhoeffer's Public Theology as Inspiration for Inter-Religious Dialogue', in *Bonhoeffer, Religion and Politics. 4th International Bonhoeffer Colloquium*, edited by Christiane Tietz and Jens Zimmerman, International Bonhoeffer Interpretations (IBI) 4 (Frankfurt am Maim: Peter Lang, 2012), 61–75.
19. Bonhoeffer, *DBWE* 8, 229–30.
20. Bonhoeffer, *DBWE* 6, 58.
21. Bonhoeffer, *DBWE* 6, 66–67.
22. Bonhoeffer, *DBWE* 4, 214.

This squares with his concept of *Christuswirklichkeit* where nought exists outside of Christ and that it is impossible, too, to be outside of Christ's saving grace. We can now interpret this to be a validation of Earth and all her ecologies, systems, and species.

In 'Thy Kingdom Come—The Prayer of the Church Community for God's Kingdom on Earth' (19 November 1932), Bonhoeffer reiterates the type of worldliness in which followers of Christ are to engage, in both spatial and temporal terms, reflecting the incarnational Christology that he was writing in the same period. When Bonhoeffer exhorts his hearers to pray, in the Lord's Prayer, 'Thy kingdom come', he emphasises the 'this-worldliness' of Christianity. 'Otherworldliness', either in the form of a future heaven or another Earth, demonstrates, for Bonhoeffer, an intrinsic disbelief in God's kingdom and in turn reflects our distorted relationship with Earth. In 'Thy Kingdom Come', Bonhoeffer is already utilising themes he would later develop in *Ethics*, that 'there are not two realities, but only one reality, and that is God's reality revealed in Christ in the reality of the world . . . The reality of Christ embraces the reality of the world in itself.'[23]

'Otherworldliness', he says in 'Thy Kingdom Come', 'is the devious trick of being religious'.[24] Focusing on a future world 'legitimises' disengagement from the harsh reality of this one, and avoids ethical engagement and the costly aspect of discipleship. Bonhoeffer challenges the false dichotomies of piety and action, and of otherworldliness from full engagement with this world. Such engagement has temporal and spatial aspects. This-worldliness places value on the present: Christ has entered into history in order to validate the present, albeit penultimate, age. Revelation breaks into all totalising systems of thought, including otherworldliness and piety. Bonhoeffer's eschatology is a fulfilment of that which has been commenced rather than a replacement for the world's apparent inadequacy. When we pray 'Thy kingdom come', we affirm the inauguration of God's kingdom and its ultimate fulfilment, and leave ourselves no option but to participate in Christ's work.

In the *Anthropocene*, eschatologies that rely on a destruction of this world in order to usher in a new world generally serve to either ignore or repudiate climate change, or at worst, welcome climate

---

23. Bonhoeffer, *DBWE* 6, 58.
24. Bonhoeffer, *DBWE* 12, 286.

change as a means to expedite the return of the Lord.[25] Bonhoeffer's 'eschatology' of this-worldliness instead fully validates the present age, requiring that we wrestle with its demands. The 'devious religious trick' of piety removes us from having to address the worldly problem of climate change and adds a cloak of respectability. In what seems paradoxical, the temporality of Christian hope necessarily bears in on the existential question for the viability of life on Earth, here and now. Whilst Bonhoeffer's seminal issue was not global warming but rather the rise of Nazism, the imperative to live faithfully and in a fully engaged way that underpins Bonhoeffer's call to discipleship is equally applicable in our own crisis. Our hope in this time of crisis relies on the unified Christ-reality 'that has been drawn into and held together in Christ'. Bonhoeffer's summary is this: 'that history moves only from this center and toward this center.'[26]

It is remarkable that one of his most well-known comments from prison so closely resembles these early questions from 'Thy Kingdom Come', one that is especially relevant in the *Anthropocene*:

> What keeps gnawing at me is the question, what is Christianity, or who is Christ actually for us today? . . . How do we speak . . . in a 'worldly' way about 'God'? How do we go about being 'religionless–worldly' Christians, how can we be ἐκ-κλησία, those who are called out, without understanding ourselves religiously as privileged, but instead seeing ourselves as belonging wholly to the world? Christ would then no longer be the object of religion, but something else entirely, truly lord of the world.[27]

What has been generally accepted as Bonhoeffer's creative prison theology can be seen to derive its foundations from his early Christology lectures, as well as to his later *Ethics* and, as shown here, 'Thy Kingdom Come'. The significance in the Anthropocene is that a unified reality of Christ-in-the-world, embracing the world-in-itself, allows us to theologically consider our relationship to Earth and her creatures as an extension of our intrinsic sociality which, in itself, is a

25. Brian McCammack, 'Hot Damned America: Evangelicalism and the Climate Change Policy Debate', in *American Quarterly,* 59/3, Religion and Politics in the Contemporary United States (2007): 645–68.
26. Bonhoeffer, *DBWE* 6, 58.
27. Bonhoeffer, *DBWE* 8, 362, 64–5.

manifestation of *Imago Dei*. That is to say that, created in the image of the Trinitarian God, we recognise that our propensity to relationships with each other and the church-community is the fullest reflection of this image. Our reconciled and restored vertical relationship with God becomes the *analogia relationis*[28] for potential horizontal relationships with others. The ecological network of co-dependent relationships throughout the biosphere, of which we are a component, can be theologically interpreted as an authentic extension of our sociality and therefore a different way of interpreting our place and role in creation becomes possible. As we recognise the immanent Christ throughout all of creation, not only in the 'face of the other [person]', we begin to perceive our own Christ-woven relationships throughout the biosphere.

Earth as our Mother

Such Christology validates the materiality of the human form derived, according to Bonhoeffer, from both *Imago Dei* and from Mother Earth:

> Humankind created in this way is humankind as the image of God. It is the image of God not in spite of but precisely in its bodily nature. For in their bodily nature human beings are related to the earth and to other bodies; they are there for others and are dependent upon others. In their bodily existence human beings find their brothers and sisters and find the earth. As such creatures human beings of earth and spirit are 'like' God, their Creator.[29]

Reading this passage through a contemporary ecological frame, Bonhoeffer can be seen as pre-empting what is now understood as the interdependence of species that comprises the biosphere. A theology that incorporates sociality that extends across species divisions and, indeed, throughout the entirety of creation, stands in contrast to less useful theologies of stewardship and dominion. These have been discussed elsewhere,[30] but such discussions tend to approach the issue

---

28. Bonhoeffer, *DBWE* 1, 58; *DBWE* 3, 65.
29. Bonhoeffer, *DBWE* 3, 79.
30. See Peter Manley Scott, 'Beyond Stewardship? Dietrich Bonhoeffer on Nature', in *Journal of Beliefs and Values* 18/2 (1997): 193–202.

from a deficit model rather than a Bonhoefferian one that provides such a positive account of creation's intrinsic relatedness.

Bonhoeffer references our relationship with Mother Earth in several more places. Consider this image from his Good Friday sermon of 1927:

> The crown, a wreath of sharp thorns, is pressed upon his forehead. The first drops of blood fall on the earth, upon which he, the love of God, walked. The earth drinks the blood of its creator's beloved Son, who loved it as no one had loved it before.[31]

Furthermore, in his exegesis of the Genesis creation story, Bonhoeffer describes Adam being taken from the Earth as we are taken from our Mother's womb; therefore, our bond with Earth is essential to our humanity and, according to Bonhoeffer, even Darwin could not have used stronger language.[32] These Earthy bodies are not the shells to simply house our spirits. Bonhoeffer says that the human being *is* a body, in a move pre-empting embedded cognition. We do not have a body and a soul; rather, we *are* a body and soul[33], making our materiality, like Christ's own materiality, implicit in what it means to be human. Bonhoeffer says 'we are a piece of Earth called by God to have human existence' and that 'what is to be taken seriously about human existence is its bond with mother earth, its being as body'.[34] Our materiality connects us to Mother Earth, 'Earth, which is the mother of us all' (Sir 40:1).[35]

Bonhoeffer supports this notion by enlisting imagery from the Greek myth of Antaeus in the Barcelona lecture, 'Basic Questions for a Christian Ethic'[36] and elsewhere.[37] Antaeus is a giant whose parents are Mother Earth, Gaea, and his father, Poseidon, the Sea, a giant who derives his special strength precisely through his physical connection to his Mother Earth. If he is ever injured, he lies down on the bare Earth and recovers and so is undefeatable, as Heracles

31. Bonhoeffer, *DBWE* 9, 520.
32. Bonhoeffer, *DBWE* 3, 76.
33. Bonhoeffer, *DBWE* 3, 7677.
34. Bonhoeffer, *DBWE* 3, 77.
35. Bonhoeffer, *DBWE* 12, 289.
36. Bonhoeffer, *DBWE* 10, 359.
37. Bonhoeffer, *DBWE* 6, 411; *DBWE* 7, 69.

(Hercules) discovers. When Heracles realises the source of Antaeus' strength, he bearhugs him, lifting him up and severing his contact with his Mother Earth unto his death. The idea of deriving strength, and perhaps morality, from Earth continues throughout Bonhoeffer's writing. Bonhoeffer's use of terms such as 'being grounded', 'standing firm' and 'having one's feet on the ground' in the Tegel 'Drama' and 'After Ten Years',[38] carry not just the metaphorical meaning of pragmatism. It could be that, in such language, he was subverting the Nazi use of the slogan, '*Blut und Boden*' (blood and soil) that had seduced the mainstream church. Perhaps, too, he was alluding to the literal meaning of physical connection to the ground beneath our feet, of the Earth rejuvenating us as we reconnect.

Connecting with Earth's energy is a feature of the Jain and Hindu spirituality of Gandhi that interested Bonhoeffer.[39] Gandhi's exhortation to 'tread lightly' resonates as not only a metaphor for leaving little trace of human presence but as a concrete way to consider what Jain spirituality understands to be the sensory perception of Earth herself. A similar notion is echoed in the Qu'ran (Sura 25: 63a), 'The true servants of the Merciful One are those who walk on the earth gently' (in other translations, 'humbly'). This verse also highlights that being faithful is equated with treading lightly. It is no coincidence therefore that, at the United Nations COP23, when the Interfaith Climate Statement on Sustainable Lifestyle was presented, it was titled 'Walk Gently on Earth'.

Towards a Bonhoefferian Ecoethic

What does it mean to walk gently, to walk humbly? I suggest the elements of an ecoethic are found in Bonhoeffer's ethical notions of *Stellvertretung* and *Sachgemaßheit*. Obedience to the person of Christ in the Anthropocene requires us to participate in 'vicarious representative action' (*Stellvertretung*) as is appropriate and necessary for this particular context (*Sachgemaßheit*). Bonhoeffer reminds us now, as then, that 'What is at stake are the times and places that pose concrete

---

38. Bonhoeffer, *DBWE* 7, 68; *DBWE* 8, 38.
39. Dianne Rayson and Terence Lovat, 'Lord of the Warming World': Bonhoeffer's Eco-Theological Ethic and the Gandhi Factor', *The Bonhoeffer Legacy: Australasian Journal of Bonhoeffer Studies* 2/1 (2012): 57–74.

questions to us, set us tasks, and lay responsibilities on us'.[40] Our ethical engagement with the climate crisis, if we were to take Bonhoeffer's lead, would require us to be conformed to God's will through a certain mindfulness of how justice and grace might exert themselves in this new age.[41] As ethical agents, we engage in a fully embodied way, and for us this may necessitate an examination of how to feed and clothe our bodies, how we transport them, how we warm them, and whether such decisions are made for the sake of the vulnerable or in spite of them. Our context is like no other, but never before has our ethical decision making been as crucial to the survival of others.

The relationship between the will and the body in ethical action reinforces the broader case being made that the overarching nature of the ecotheological question is one of sociality. Sociality, in this context, relates not only to the human species in the way classically articulated by Green.[42] The critical aspect of Bonhoeffer's theology in relation to the ecotheological question is that sociality, to be fully manifest, must extend to the entire Earth community. An apparent shortcoming in public theology has been in a poor articulation of our ethical relationships with the other-than-human Earthlings. Following Bonhoeffer, basing that ethical relationship on notions of *Stellvertretung* and *Sachgemäßheit* would logically direct our action in the climate crisis in favour of those at significant risk. The evidence demonstrates that this includes the poorest of the human race, vulnerable ecosystems, and critically endangered species.

An ethical imperative such as articulated above has sound theological foundations in Bonhoeffer's Christology, one that reflects the trifold forms of Christ, one that reflects the trifold forms of Christ as human, crucified and resurrected and as such affirms God's love for creation, judgement, and reconciliation.[43] Christology of this type validates the materiality of the human form derived both from the image of God and from Mother Earth:

> Humankind created in this way is humankind as the image of God. It is the image of God not in spite of but precisely

---

40. Bonhoeffer, *DBWE* 6, 101.
41. Bonhoeffer, *DBWE* 10, 365.
42. Clifford J Green, *Bonhoeffer: A Theology of Sociality*, revised edition (Grand Rapids: Eerdmans, 1999).
43. Bonhoeffer, *DBWE* 6, 157.

in its bodily nature. For in their bodily nature human beings are related to the earth and to other bodies; they are there for others and are dependent upon others. In their bodily existence human beings find their brothers and sisters and find the earth. As such creatures human beings of earth and spirit are 'like' God, their Creator.[44]

Several notes from prison written around July–August 1944 provide evidence that Bonhoeffer was engaging with non-religious interpretations of Christian concepts and how they might translate into a new world. His note, 'what if Christianity was not a religion at all?' might serve as an impetus for a religionless Christianity which is outward looking and operates on behalf of the vulnerable, so enacting our 'belonging wholly to the world'. Bonhoeffer was anticipating the move toward a non-religious encounter with the God who suffers with creation. Such a tendency finds its fulfilment in the human turn toward Earth. Participating in the manifestation of God's kingdom on Earth is only possible for those who see Christ both in Earth, and for Earth: *In Mundo, Pro Mundo*. In a letter to his fiancée, Bonhoeffer succinctly combines the ethical imperative with judgement, saying, 'Our marriage must be a "yes" to God's earth. . . . I fear that Christians who venture to stand on earth on only one leg will stand in heaven on only one leg too.'[45] Standing with Earth becomes a manifestation of becoming, not *Homo religiosus*, as Bonhoeffer argued against,[46] but becoming more fully human.

I propose that the term *Homo cosmicos* reflects such a notion of becoming more 'fully human'. It better recognises the interrelatedness of humanity with all of creation, both ecologically and theologically. The use of *Homo cosmicos*, in this way, reflects both meanings in Latin of 'belonging to the world' and being 'a citizen of the world'.

Bonhoeffer's attention to belonging to Earth and to responsible action are reflected in both types of meaning in the term *Homo cosmicos*. In both senses, it would appear to be a useful, positive way to describe the fully human being as we approach the ecoethical chal-

---

44. Bonhoeffer, *DBWE* 3, 79.
45. Ruth-Alice von Bismarck and Ulrich Kabitz, editors, *Love Letters from Cell 92: The Correspondence between Dietrich Bonhoeffer and Maria Von Wedemeyer 1943–45* (Nashville: Abingdon, 1995), 64.
46. Bonhoeffer, *DBWE* 2, 162; *DBWE* 6, 357; *DBWE* 8, 188.

lenges ahead. *Homo cosmicos* encapsulates the idea of vulnerability that is required of the Christian disciple seeking to participate with Christ in Earth's suffering. The task of the sentient, loving species is to devote intelligence and love, and indeed our wills and our bodies, to the entire Earth community. According to Bonhoeffer,

> Only when one loves life and the Earth so much that with it everything seems to be lost and at its end may one believe in the resurrection of the dead and a new world.[47]

Conclusion

Loving life and Earth becomes constitutive of the validated human experience that Bonhoeffer both articulated and demonstrated. It also provides the way forward in a journey to reclaim Christian hope in an era devoid of security and promise. Earthly Christianity, then, provides a way to speak in a 'religionless-worldly' voice that reflects our ecological integration in the biosphere and our particular responsibility to it. When we understand ourselves as belonging wholly to the world, we sense both the task and the obligation required of us in the *Anthropocene.*

---

47. Bonhoeffer, *DBWE* 8, 213.

Dietrich Bonhoeffer's Stand on the Jewish Question during the Third Reich

John Moses

Introduction

Dietrich Bonhoeffer's reputation, as far as the secular world is concerned, is based on his well-known opposition to the Nazi regime and the martyrdom he suffered because of it. Less well known is the fact that Bonhoeffer's motivation for joining in the conspiracy to overthrow Hitler was his revulsion at Nazi Jewish policy and his repudiation and revision of the anti-Judaistic theology prevalent in his church practically since Luther's time.[1] While Luther's enunciation of the theology of justification had established the so-called Protestant principle and thus given the non-Roman and non-Orthodox Christian world an irrefutable *raison d'être*, Luther also bequeathed to his church a stubborn anti-Judaistic theology that demanded Jews submit to baptism or be driven out of the land.[2] That Bonhoeffer's revolutionary theology and its significance is not very well understood is evidenced by the fact that no less a scholar than Saul Friedlaender in 1997 could accuse Bonhoeffer of an unreconstructed theological anti-Semitism that is assumed to have 'moulded some of his pronouncements' on the Jewish question.[3]

Friedlaender based his judgement on a single article, not primarily about Bonhoeffer but about his co-religionist Martin Niemöller.[4] In a

---

1. John A Moses, *Reluctant Revolutionary: Dietrich Bonhoeffer's Collision with Prusso-German History* (New York/Oxford: Berghahn Books 2009).
2. Jan Herman Brinks, 'Luther and the German State', in *The Heythrop Journal,* 38 (1998): 1–17.
3. Saul Friedlander, *Nazi Germany and the Jews,* vol. I, *The Years of Persecution, 1933–1939* (New York: Harper Collins, 1997), 45.
4. Robert Michael, 'Theological Myth, German Anti-Semitism and the Holocaust: The Case of Martin Niemöller, in *Holocaust and Genocide Studies,* 2/1 (1987): 105–22.

topic so fraught with emotion and prejudice, this kind of scholarship serves only to re-enforce stereotypes. While it is true that Bonhoeffer was a product of the *Bildungsbürgertum* and a theological tradition that was fundamentally anti-Judaistic, his merit consists in the fact that he was uniquely able to repudiate the prejudice of his class and the theological errors of his mentors. Friedlaender could not have fallen so embarrassingly into such an error of judgement as he did if he had taken the trouble to consult Eberhard Bethge's 1962 biography of Bonhoeffer and his later study, 'Bonhoeffer und die Juden' from 1979.[5] Here one learns how Bonhoeffer went through a learning process before arriving at his revolutionary pro-Jewish theology that has placed the post-war Christian-Jewish dialogue onto a totally new and eirenical plane.

The Anti-Semitic background

In order to gauge the height of Bonhoeffer's achievement in this regard we need to be aware of the depth of anti-Semitism in European history generally and in modern German history in particular. Religious anti-Judaism from Luther's time up to the nineteenth century certainly laid the foundation for secular anti-Semitism, a movement that had a number of champions of varying degrees of rabidity that ranged from demanding the expulsion of Jews from Germany to their physical extermination.[6]

The rationale for these measures was that the presence of Jews in German society was deleterious both racially through intermarriage, and socially, because the Jewish mentality and mores, especially those of secular Jews, eroded true Christian and Teutonic values. Indeed, in the 1890's the court preacher, Adolf Stoecker, actually founded an anti-Semitic political party based on these views. That this party was only short-lived was not due to its anti-Semitism but rather to the fact

---

5. Eberhard Bethge, 'Dietrich Bonhoeffer und die Juden', in Heinz Kremer, editor *Die Juden und Martin Luther: Martin Luther und die Juden* (Vluyn: Neukirchener Verlagsgesellschaft, 1988). See also Victoria Barnett's revised edition of Bethge's, biography newly entitled, *Dietrich Bonhoeffer: A Biography* (Minneapolis: Fortress Pres, 2000), 271–279. As well see, John D Godsey & Geffrey B Kelly, *Ethical Responsibility: Bonhoeffer's Legacy to the Churches* (New York: Edwin Mellen, 1981), 43–96.

6. Peter Pulzer, *The Rise of Political Anti-Semitism* (Harvard University Press, 1998).

it had no social programme that could attract voters away from the existing mainstream parties.[7]

The reality was that anti-Semitism did not need a political party to propagate it. It was deeply entrenched in the *völkisch* mentality of the time, and even in the more highly refined circles of the *Bildungsbürgertum*.[8]

The concept of *Bildung*, as Fritz Ringer has shown, when closely examined, was predicated on a quite blatantly racist premise. Essentially, *Bildung*, meaning formation as a cultivated individual, could only occur if one was of German blood. Persons of non-German race were thus ruled out of contention since they did not possess the essential biological/spiritual equipment necessary to become truly *gebildet*.[9]

Obviously, this concept was not loudly proclaimed until after the Nazi seizure of power because numerous high-profile German-Jews in all spheres of learning and the arts can be named who perceived themselves as *Bildungsbürger*. And certainly not all Aryan *Bildungsbürger* were anti-Semitic as both sides of Bonhoeffer's family attested.

Nevertheless, as he observed after 1933, Bonhoeffer was astonished how many *Bildungsbürger* compliantly served in the Nazi bureaucracy assisting to implement the anti-Jewish policy. Indeed, what worried him was not so much the anti-Semitism of the rank and file of the Nazi party but that of the educated class who should have known better. As he remarked in a letter to his Swiss friend Erwin Sutz, these people had lost both their heads and their Bibles.[10] Why such people had failed to 'open their mouth for the dumb' and preferred to bludgeon their conscience into submission, silently wit-

---

7. On Adolf Stoecker see, Gunter Brakelmann, Martin Greschat & Werner Jochmann, *Protestantismus und Politik: Werke und Wirkung Adolf Stoeckers* (Hamburg: Christians Verlag, 1982).

8. Suspicion and hostility towards Jews goes back to the very origins of the Church. See my chapter, 'The Problem of Anti-Semitism in Germany from Luther to Hitler', 46–72 in *The Reluctant Revolutionary*, referenced footnote 1. Specifically on Roman Catholic anti-Semitism see John Connelly, *From Enemy to Brother: The Revolution in Catholic Teaching on the Jews 1933–1965* (Cambridge, Mass/London: Harvard University Press, 2012).

9. Fritz Ringer, '"*Bildung*": The Social and Ideological Context of the German Historical Tradition', in *History of European Ideas*, 10/ 2 (1989): 193–202.

10. Bonhoeffer to Erwin Sutz, 14 April 1933 in volume12, 'Berlin 1932–1933' (Minneapolis: Fortress Press, 2009), 59. 'The Jewish question is also giving the church a great deal of trouble, and here the most intelligent people have totally lost both their heads and their Bible', Bonhoeffer, *DBWE* 12, 99–100.

nessing criminal acts on a massive scale, was ultimately a question of character and faith.[11]

The issue of anti-Judaism in the church was, on the other hand, essentially one of a falsely understood theology among clergy who were seduced into acquiescence with the Nazi policy of exclusion of so-called non-Aryans from the national community.[12] This is a commentary on the virulence of racial dogmas, the myth of Aryan superiority and the belief that the presence of Jews in the community was deleterious. High profile churchmen such as Otto Dibelius (1880–1967), for example, were quite frank about their anti-Judaistic theology and anti-Semitism.[13] They prioritised, in fact, the doctrine of the uniqueness and purity of the *Volk* over the clear Biblical teaching that in Christ differences of race, gender and social status were irrelevant.[14]

When the church was confronted with taking a stand on the Nazi Aryan legislation in April 1933, Bonhoeffer was alarmed. He had to oppose the policy to exclude from the pastorate all clergy who were converts from Judaism in the same way as the state excluded persons of Jewish origin from the public service. This was an issue entailing a most crucial theological principle. Within two weeks of the Prus-

---

11. Bonhoeffer reflected on this very central problem in his essay, 'After Ten years' written at the end of 1942 for his circle of friends. It is a penetrating critique of his own class, the *Bildungsbürgertum* and rewards a close reading. See Bonhoeffer, *DBWE* 8, translated as 'An Account at the Turn of the Year 1942–1943: After Ten Years', 37–52.

12. This subject is treated in detail by Ian Kershaw, *Hitler*, volume I: *1889–1936 Hubris* (London: Penguin, 1998), 474, 504.

13. On Dibelius see, John Conway, *The Nazi Persecution of the Churches 1933–45* (London: Weidenfeld & Nicolson, 1968), 32, 342–4, 420–1,400; Richard Steigmann-Gall, *The Holy Reich: Nazi Conceptions of Christianity 1919–1945* (Cambridge University Press, 2004).

14. The literature on this subject is considerable, but see, Robert P Ericksen and Susannah Heschel, editors, *Betrayal: German Churches and the Holocaust* (Minneapolis: Augsburg Fortress Press, 1999); therein, Robert P Ericksen, 'Assessing the Heritage: German Protestant Theologians and the "Jewish Question"', 22–39. The classic Biblical locus of the universalism of the teachings of Jesus is in St Paul's Epistle to the Galatians, chapter 3 verses 25–29: 'But now that faith has come, we are no longer under a custodian; for in Christ Jesus you are all sons of God, through faith. For as many of you were baptized into Christ have put on Christ. There is neither Jew nor Greek, there is neither slave nor free, there is neither male nor female; for you are all one in Christ Jesus. And if you are Christ's, then you are Abraham's offspring, heirs according to promise.'

sian Synod endorsing the Aryan paragraph for the church, Bonhoeffer wrote, and soon after published, his first public statement on the 'Church and the Jewish Question'.[15] It contained some ambivalent passages about the Jews as a people both loved and cursed by God, but ultimately demanded that the state cease to persecute a defenceless minority because to do so was an abuse of state power, and secondly, the paper demanded that the church not only had the duty to bind up the wounds of those crushed, as it were, under the wheel of the state, but had to consider whether to put a spoke in the wheel. This was the first visible evidence in Bonhoeffer's writing that he was thinking of the possibility of active resistance against a regime that he clearly regarded as illegitimate.[16]

Bonhoeffer's stand

During 1933 Bonhoeffer was actively engaged in getting the church to make an unequivocal stand against both Nazi church policy[17] that was supporting the aberrant *Deutsche Christen* (German Christians) who openly celebrated Hitler as the new saviour, and against the acceptance in the wider church of the Aryan paragraph. Getting co-religionists to take a stand against the German Christians was comparatively easy because traditional Lutherans were strong on the doctrine-of-the-two-kingdoms (*die Zweireichelehre*) that insisted on the complete autonomy of the church to preach the Gospel without interference from the state. Bonhoeffer's ally, Martin Niemöller,

---

15. See the English translation in Bonhoeffer, *DBWE*, 12, 361–370. in footnote 14. See also Ruther Zerner, 'Church, State and the Jewish Question', in *The Cambridge Companion to Dietrich Bonhoeffer* edited by John W de Gruchy (Cambridge University Press, 1999), 190–205. Zerner draws attention to early statements by Bonhoeffer in 1934, that indicate that he was still very much anchored in the Lutheran tradition of according to the State a God-given vocation to represent the authority of almighty God on earth. He eventually came to the view that the National Socialist regime was in fact no real state at all in the Lutheran sense. See John A Moses, 'Church and State on post-Reformation Germany, 1530–1914', in *Church and State in Old and New Worlds,* edited by Hilary M Cary and John Gascoigne (Leiden: Brill, 2011), 77–98.
16. Bonhoeffer, *DBWE* 12, 225.
17. *Cf* Michael DeJonge, *Bonhoeffer's Reception of Luther* (Oxford: Oxford University Press, 2017), and Heinz Tödt, *Authentic Faith: Bonhoeffer's Theological Ethics in Context* (Grand Rapids: ET Eerdmans, 2007).

founded the Pastors' Emergency League that confronted the German Christians precisely because they violated the Reformation formularies of Martin Luther and the unity of Holy Scripture. The League also repudiated the Aryan paragraph as a further violation of the Reformation confession because of the theological principles that Jews could be baptised (indeed, ought to be) and able then to participate fully in the communion of the faithful.[18] One could not deny the fact that the first Christians were baptized Jews.

What is interesting, however, is that whereas the Pastors' Emergency League could command a considerable following among the clergy by the end of 1933 on the principles enunciated, and thus became the foundation of the future Confessing Church in Germany, it never followed through on its repudiation of the Aryan paragraph. That is to say, their opposition to the Nazis was really based more on a determination to uphold traditional Lutheran teaching with regard to the state; they were far less enthusiastic about standing up in practice for the rights of baptised Jews, not to mention the non-baptised Jews. In short, even in the Confessing Church the majority of pastors were still anti-Judaistic in their theology. They were committed to the belief that the 'New Covenant' ushered in by Christ had completely abrogated the 'Old Covenant' between God and Moses, and that because the Jews were responsible for the crucifixion of Christ, having refused to recognise him as their Messiah, they incurred the wrath of God and had suffered throughout history the consequences of this rejection. And, indeed, what was happening to the Jews under the Nazis was interpreted as nothing more or less than the fulfilment of Jesus' prophecy in Matthew 23: 29–36 that begins, 'Woe to you scribes and Pharisees, hypocrites!' and continues, 'Serpents, brood of vipers! How can you escape the condemnation of hell?' And further states: 'that on you may come all the righteous blood on the earth . . .' [. . .] 'Assuredly, I say to you, all these things will come upon this generation.'[19]

---

18. On the question of the baptising of Jews and the attitude of the Nazi-oriented "German Christians", see Doris L Bergen, *Twisted Cross: The German Christian Movement in the Third Reich* (Chapel Hill: University of North Carolina Press, 1996), 85–93.

19. Conway, *Nazi Persecution*, 78–87; Asta von Oppen, *Der unerhörte Schrei; Dietrich Bonhoeffer und die Judenfrage im Dritten Reich* (Hannover: Lutherisches Verlagshaus, 1996), 67–79.

Bonhoeffer came to find any kind of preaching based on an uncritical reception of these passages to be based on an extremely dubious theology—he was 'shedding his skin'. As he developed Bonhoeffer came to understand that the ethical thrust of the Bible was to emphasise the *diaconal* role of the church; its function to protect the persecuted, and if necessary, to suffer along with them, in short, 'to open thy mouth for the dumb' (Prov 31: 8–9). And indeed, Bonhoeffer was engaged in doing precisely that as pastor in London from October 1933 until April 1935 ministering to the German-Jewish refugees.[20]

On 15 September 1935 the so-called Nuremberg Laws were promulgated that defined who was to be regarded as a Jew in Germany on the basis of an individual's Jewish ancestry. Later that month the Synod of Berlin-Steglitz was to debate the Aryan paragraph, and this presented Bonhoeffer and his students with the opportunity to agitate for the church to take a stand against the state on behalf of non-Aryan Christians. A memorandum for this purpose was prepared and tabled at the Synod. It elicited only a weak response in which the Synod merely affirmed that no Jew was to be denied the sacrament of baptism and that the charity of Christ was to be exercised towards the non-baptised Jews. It reflected, in fact, the fear of the church of the consequence of new Nazi regulations to monitor the finances of the church and to interfere in its internal affairs.[21]

Bonhoeffer, though, saw in this a further capitulation before a fraudulent regime and evidence of a bankruptcy of theology in the Confessing Church that had again missed an opportunity to put a spoke in the wheel of the state. The church was clearly incapable of 'opening its mouth for the dumb'. Its repeated failure to do this caused Bonhoeffer to query, 'Are we still the church of the ever-present Christ?' Only a few colleagues were listening because within three months of the promulgation of the Nuremberg Laws, the Confessing Church leadership was appealing to affiliated parishes to celebrate the centenary of the birth of the anti-Semitic pastor, Adolf Stoecker.[22] This was to affirm the widespread belief that Jews were a deleterious influence within German society. Here the tendency to 'howl with the wolves' was predominant.

---

20. Bethge, *Dietrich Bonhoeffer* (2000), 277.
21. Bethge, *Dietrich Bonhoeffer* (2000), 413–14.
22. von Oppen, *Der Unerhörte Schrei*, 70.

On the other hand, there were elements within the Confessing Church who were prepared to send a memorandum to Hitler complaining that the state was forcing the church to hatred of the Jews and that this was a violation of the commandment to love one's neighbour. Two of the formulators of this memorandum were, not surprisingly, former students of Bonhoeffer, but they paid for their efforts by serving the next two years in a concentration camp. The senior signatory, Friedrich Weissler, was murdered in a concentration camp.[23]

Clearly, the church was being warned not to 'open its mouth for the dumb' under any circumstances, and many pastors actually preached anti-Judaistic sermons to ingratiate themselves with the regime. Bonhoeffer, though, persisted in developing a theology that overcame the seemingly unbridgeable gulf separating church and Synagogue. He did this by locating the two in a reciprocal relationship whereby the church should have permanently in mind its Jewish roots from which it could not be separated. His Biblical source was St Paul's Epistle to the Romans 11:17–18.

> Some of the branches of the cultivated olive tree have been broken off, and a branch of a wild olive tree has been joined to it. You gentiles are like that wild olive tree, and now you share the strong spiritual life of the Jews. So, then, you must not despise those who were broken off like those who were broken like branches. How can you be proud? You are just a branch; you don't support the roots. The roots support you.[24]

The logic of this assessment was patently clear to Bonhoeffer, but ignored by most of the co-religionists. Then, on the night of 9 November 1938, the program known as *Reichskristallnacht* (night of broken glass) was carried out, ordered by propaganda minister Josef Goebbels, in which synagogues were burned, Jewish-owned businesses destroyed and many Jews killed and arrested. Bonhoeffer marked his Bible at Psalm 74, verse 8: 'They want to crush us completely;

---

23. Ferdinand Schlingensiepen, *Dietrich Bonhoeffer 1906–1945: Eine Biographie* (München: Verlag CH Beck, 2005), 218. Now in English translation by Isabel Best, *Dietrich Bonhoeffer 1906–1945: Martyr, Thinker, Man of Resistance* (London: T&T Clark, 2010).

24. See a full discussion of this subject in John A Moses, *The Reluctant Revolutionary,* Chapter 7, 'Bonhoeffer and the Jewish Question' on pages 148–172, but especially 157–158.

they burnt down every holy place in the land.' But again the majority of Lutheran theologians saw in these events the proof that the Jews had been cursed for having rejected Christ. Bonhoeffer, on the other hand, predicted that, 'If today the synagogues burn, tomorrow the churches will be set on fire'.[25] Bonhoeffer now reversed the traditional criticism of Israel by the church into a criticism of the church for failing to take the part of what he called the persecuted Jewish brothers of Jesus. Indeed, only a church that did so would be consistent with the Jewishness of Jesus and aware of the significance which his people had for him.

Bonhoeffer's enduring influence

Gradually, some pastors experienced a change of heart and began to preach in accordance with Bonhoeffer's ideas. But this inevitably led to their arrest and imprisonment. The church had finally realised that there could be no compromise with the regime, and at a church rally in Berlin-Steglitz on 10–12 December 1938 a communiqué was released that protested against the arrest of pastors and at the same time urged solidarity with converted Jews, calling them brothers and sisters, for the very first time.[26] This had been a stern learning process for the church. Initially in 1933 it showed only a desire to be rid of Jews entirely. Five years later pastors faced the reality of imprisonment for speaking out for them. If the church in 1933 had taken on board what Bonhoeffer had urged as the role of the church, namely to admonish the state of its duty towards all citizens regardless of race, the situation could conceivably have developed differently. But given the deeply embedded tradition of the Lutheran Church in Germany of unconditional obedience to the Powers-that-be, the idea of assuming the role of conscience of the state was utopian. Similarly, the idea that the church under certain circumstances might initiate active opposition and put a spoke in the wheel of the state was beyond comprehension at the time. Bonhoeffer occupied a lonely outpost.

---

25. von Oppen, *Der unerhörte Schrei*, 77; *Cf* Bethge, *Dietrich Bonhoeffer* (2000), 607, and 'Dietrich Bonhoeffer und de Juden', 237. John A Moses, *The Reluctant Revolutionary*, 158.
26. von Oppen, *Der unerhörte Schrei*, 78–79.

By 1939, Bonhoeffer had finally assessed the situation as requiring more drastic intervention. Agitation through the church, even training ordination candidates in his Finkenwalde Seminary, was not enough. The ecclesiastical reformer had to become a political conspirator having been introduced to the resistance movement by his brother-in-law, Hans von Dohnanyi. Bonhoeffer became literally a double agent whose cover was working for the German military counter-intelligence, the *Abwehr*. By virtue of his new status he was exempted from military service and could travel abroad on official business. These trips to Switzerland and Sweden and even to Italy were opportunities for contact with the representatives of the ecumenical movement, and through them he learned of the first transport of Jews to concentration camps. That was to Gurs in the South of France in October 1940 where over six thousand had been transported.[27] Deportations to the east began only after the Russian campaign had started as areas for possible re-settlement of Jews were conquered. These occurred between 29 August and 26 September 1941.[28]

Between his duties as an agent Bonhoeffer was able to continue his work, suggested by the Council of Brethren of the Confessing Church (*Brüderrat*) on a systematic study of Protestant ethics. He had already come to the awareness that the hatred of Jews having been instituted by the state had become official government policy. Bonhoeffer was honest and astute enough to grasp that this hatred had its roots in the history of the church and its theological distortions. These he now set out to correct and he did it by re-evaluating the course of the history of the West, seeing it as a continuity of Jewish history.[29] They key passage in *Ethics* is a follows:

> The historical Jesus is the continuity of our history. But Jesus Christ was the promised Messiah of the Israelite-Jewish people, and for that reason the line of our forefathers goes back beyond the appearance of Jesus to the people of Israel.

---

27. Bethge, *Dietrich Bonhoeffer* (2000), 728.
28. See *The Holocaust Encyclopedia*, edited by Walter Laqueur and Judith Tydor Baumel (New Haven/London: Yale University Press, entry *Gurs*. Note: In addition, between 6 August, 1942 and 3 March 1943, Vichy French officials turn over 3,907 Jewish prisoners from Gurs to the Germans.
29. See Henry Mottu, *Bonhoeffer* (Paris: Cerf: 2002), 99–103, where Mottu identifies three phases in Bonhoeffer's developing understanding of the Jewish question in the history of the German Lutheran church.

Western history is by God's will, indissolubly linked with the people of Israel, not only genetically but also in a genuine uninterrupted encounter. The Jews keep open the question of Christ. They are the sign of the free mercy-choice and the repudiating wrath of God: 'Behold, therefore, the goodness and severity of God' (Rom 11:22). An expulsion of the Jews from the West must necessarily bring with it the expulsion of Christ. For Jesus Christ was a Jew.[30]

This had been written after the first deportation of Jews to the East had occurred. At that stage, of course, Bonhoeffer had no idea of what would result from this as the Wannsee Conference that determined the extermination of the Jews had not taken place until January 1942. Expulsion led to annihilation, and the guilt weighed heavily on the Christian Church. Thus Bonhoeffer accused the church:

She was silent when she should have cried out because the blood of the innocent was crying aloud to heaven. She failed to speak the right word in the right way at the right time. She has not resisted to the uttermost the apostasy of faith, and she has brought upon herself the guilt of the godlessness of the masses.[31]

Certainly, there had been frequent opportunities for the church to raise its voice between the first boycott of Jewish shops in 1933 and the progrom of November 1938, but it failed to do so. There had been a catastrophic decline in faith and the thundering proof of this came in an official circular dated two days before Christmas 1941 from the Chancellery of the German Evangelical Church, advising all church offices throughout the land that the 'breakthrough of the racial idea' within the nation had required the expulsion of the Jews from the community, and in the light of this appropriate measures were to be taken to ensure that baptised non-Aryans did not participate in the life of the church. Those concerned would have to make whatever arrangements they could for church services and pastoral care.[32] This open complicity in the crimes against humanity by the official church led Bonhoeffer to demand in *Ethics*:

---

30. Dietrich Bonhoeffer, *Ethics* in *DBWE* 6, 105.
31. Bonhoeffer, *Ethics* in *DBWE* 6, 140.
32. von Oppen, *Der unerhörte Schrei*, 93.

The church confesses that it has witnessed the arbitrary use of brutal force, the suffering in body and soul of countless innocent people, that it has witnessed oppression, hatred, and murder without raising its voice for the victims and without finding ways of rushing to help them. It has become guilty of the lives of the weakest and most defenceless brothers and sisters of Jesus Christ [. . .]. The church confesses that is has looked on silently as the poor were exploited and robbed, while the strong were enriched and corrupted.[33]

Bonhoeffer's Inter-faith proposition

Whereas the Confessing Church only reserved the term 'brothers and sisters of Jesus Christ' for baptised Jews, Bonhoeffer here includes all Jews as deserving the protection of Christians. And consistent with his youthful thoughts on the nature of the church in the world, Bonhoeffer then affirms that the role of a truly penitent church would be actually to suffer in sympathy with the non-Aryan victims. As Christ suffered arrest, trial and crucifixion, the genuine discipleship of Christ meant also to enter into the community of guilt of all and to suffer the burden of that guilt. Such action would be genuine Christian responsibility. Indeed, Bonhoeffer's theology 'is a theology of responsibility for not only the church but for the entire world'.[34] And that included taking the part of the Jews, the baptised and the non-baptised, without distinction. This would be obligatory particularly because of the revised relationship between Church and Synagogue which is now seen by Bonhoeffer as one of *interdependence* whereas previously it was thought to be one of irreconcilable hostility.

The implications of this are revolutionary. The former Protestant attitude, not to mention Anglican and Roman Catholic, was that Jews had to be converted; that was the church's role in history. Hence the German Protestants had maintained their so-called *Judenmission*, the mission to the Jews whose point of departure was that the Jewish revelation on Sinai had been abrogated by the revelation in Christ.[35]

---

33. Bonhoeffer, *Ethics* in *DBWE* 6, 139–140.
34. Larry Rasmussen, 'The Ethics of Responsible Action', in *The Cambridge Companion to Dietrich Bonhoeffer*, 206–225.
35. Christopher Clark, *The Politics of Conversion: Missionary Protestantism and the Jews in Prussia, 1728–1944* (Oxford: Oxford University Press, 1995).

With Bonhoeffer this no longer made any sense because the God of the Jews was also the God of the New Testament; indeed, the God of creation was also the God of redemption. Further, the God of the Old Testament is the father of Jesus Christ and the God revealed in Jesus Christ is the God of the Old Testament. He is a triune God. As Asta von Oppen has pointed out, the Incarnation and the Cross, namely the revelation made to the gentile world, required that the Old Testament be read anew, in balance with the New Testament, otherwise humanity would be restricted to a Jewish understanding of the Old Testament. It needs to be re-read from the stand point of the Incarnation and Calvary. In short, the Christian can only comprehend the New Testament against the background of the Jewish scriptures on the one hand and on the other hand from the history of the church ever since.[36]

This raises the question whether Bonhoeffer saw the Old Testament as a mere prelude to the New. Certainly not, in the view of Asta von Oppen. His entire witness especially after the *Night of Broken Glass* was based on the insight that the church had a responsibility for all Jews. Bonhoeefer had obviously moved much closer to Karl Barth who had already warned that the God of creation and the God of redemption were one and the same and may not be separated, but at the same time one could not lose sight of the uniqueness of Christ. Bonhoeffer manages to do this by re-evaluating further the theological function of the Old Testament. This he saw as *witnessing* to God's blessing on all creation, thus affirming the validity of this worldly life. As such it gives essential ballast to the New Testament with its prioritisation of redemption and resurrection in the life beyond. In doing this Bonhoeffer sought to overcome the tradition of seeing the Old Testament as merely a prelude to the New, and thus of inferior significance.[37] As he wrote, 'The difference between the OT and the NT

---

36. A close reading of Asta von Oppen, *Der unerhörte Schrei,* 67–108 makes clear that the former conviction that the New Testament abrogated the Old Testament was utterly fallacious. Rather one has to grasp the essential complementarity of the two. Politically in the Third Reich the consequence had to be drawn that it was the church's duty to stand up for the Jews whether they were baptised or not. Von Oppen's ideas would require an independent and expansive analysis.

37. Martin Kuske, *Das alte Testament als Buch von Christus: Dietrich Bonhoeffers Auslegung und Auswertung des alten* Testaments (Berlin: Vandenhoek & Ruprecht, 1971). Andreas Pangritz, 'Who is Jesus Christ for us Today?', in *The Cambridge Companion to Dietrich Bonhoeffer,* 134–153.

in this regard lies in the fact that in the OT the blessing encompasses also the Cross while in the NT the Cross encompasses the blessing'.[38] In this way, Bonhoeffer saw both Testaments as standing in an indissoluble complementarity that made irrelevant all previous comparisons of the two that spoke of subordination or prioritisation. Such an approach then opened the way for a new sense of Christian responsibility for the people of the Old Testament, but not only for these, but for all humanity as part of creation.

Conclusion

Finally, Bonhoeffer's theological pilgrimage was clearly determined by the political circumstances of his time. The insights he won derived from responding to the challenge of the crises with which the church was daily confronted during the Third Reich. We see a committed Lutheran, deeply imbued with the content of the 'protestant' theology that Luther formulated and bequeathed, especially that regarding justification and forgiveness, but also Luther's doctrine of the two kingdoms, reacting to a godless tyranny whose self-appointed task had been to exterminate the first people of God. In confronting this unprecedented barbarism Bonhoeffer found himself having to overcome a centuries-old falsely understood Christian anti-Judaism as well as secular anti-Semitism. This task was doubly difficult because the overwhelming majority of Bonhoeffer's contemporaries both in the church and in bourgeois society generally held the anti-Judaistic and anti-Semitic beliefs as paradigmatic. In Bonhoeffer's repudiation of the latter and his re-conceptualising the Jewish-Christian relationship he had become not only a far-sighted theological pioneer but simultaneously a radical political revolutionary. And his life, witness and martyrdom has enabled a Christian-Jewish dialogue to develop in place of centuries of rejection and persecution.

---

38. von Oppen, *Der unerhörte Schrei*, 104.

Vol 6 No 1/2018

What's This Book Actually About?
Life Together and the Possibility of Theological Knowledge

Derek W Taylor

Introduction

Readers of *Life Together*[1] face an immediate question. What's this book actually *about*? Three interpretive options seem most plausible. I refer to them as (1) the ecclesiological option, (2) the pastoral option, and (3) the theological option. The first reading, the ecclesiological, is the most general. It claims that *Life Together* is a commentary on how to form authentic Christian community, on how to be the church. The second reading, the pastoral, is more specific. As Eberhard Bethge writes in his Afterword to the 1979 German edition, this book is not for families or home life but for the particular task of training aspiring pastors.[2] The third option shifts the emphasis to theological education. Finkenwalde was not merely a preacher's seminary—Bonhoeffer imagined it as something more, as a way to lead students into authentic knowledge of God.

In its reception history, the first two options have predominated. In this article I take the third approach. I propose reading *Life Together* as an essay on the possibility of theological education. This book is not merely about forming community or training pastors—it's Bonhoeffer's retrospective reflection on what it looked like for this particular community to learn to think and speak rightly about God.

1. Bonhoeffer, *DBWE* 5.
2. Eberhard Bethge, "Nachwort," in *Gemeinsames Leben* (Gütersloher Verlaghaus, 2006), translated by Geffrey B. Kelley, *International Bonhoeffer Society Newsletter*, 56 (June 1994), 9–14. For a recent example of this line of interpretation, see Paul R. House, *Bonhoeffer's Seminary Vision: A Case for Costly Discipleship and Life Together* (Wheaton, IL: Crossway, 2015).

Obstacle one

This reading faces two obvious obstacles. First, as Bethge just reminded us, Finkenwalde was, in fact, a preacher's seminary, not an academic institution. Students entered the seminary only after completing formal theological studies in the university. The exception that proves the rule is a student named Gerhard Lehne, who recalls feeling great trepidation upon entering Finkenwalde because he was the only student *without* well-formed and incisive theological positions.[3] Like other preacher's seminaries, Finkenwalde was meant to provide a practical supplement to the students' already established theological foundation. It would therefore seem obvious to read *Life Together* as an experiment in training for ministry. Hence the popularity of the second option.

It is not hard to see, however, that Bonhoeffer desired to abolish the traditional academic-pastoral divide. It is telling, for instance, that he insisted on forming a House of Brethren to exist alongside the Seminary—this suggests, at the least, that his vision of the community went beyond the seminary alone. Indeed, much of what appears in *Life Together* reflects on the unique forms of communal life that the House of Brethren made possible. We also know, as a matter of biography, that Bonhoeffer had been growing dissatisfied with his earlier treatment of theology as a 'more academic matter'. As he famously claims in a 1934 letter to his friend, Erwin Sutz, 'I no longer believe in the university, and in fact I never really did'.[4] He thus seems to be presenting Finkenwalde not merely as another preachers' seminary but as an alternative to the university itself. As he says to Karl Barth in 1936, Finkenwalde combines 'both scholarly and practical work so wonderfully'.[5] Indeed, Bonhoeffer was highly critical of the university education his students had previously received; they came to him 'empty . . . with regard to theological knowledge' and thus they needed 'a completely different kind of training'.[6] He continues, 'It is perfectly clear to me that none of these things [practical pastoral tasks] has any legitimacy if not accompanied—simultaneously!—by genuinely serious, rigorous theological, exegetical, and dogmatic work.'[7]

---

3. Bonhoeffer, *DBWE* 15, 128.
4. Bonhoeffer, *DBWE* 13, 217.
5. Bonhoeffer, *DBWE* 14, 253.
6. Bonhoeffer, *DBWE* 14, 253.
7. Bonhoeffer, *DBWE* 14, 254.

Obstacle two

The second obstacle is more formidable. On matters of theological education, *Life Together* is silent. The book doesn't actually say anything about theological study. The only time the word 'study' shows up it is negated. When we read the Bible, Bonhoeffer suggests, we are explicitly *not* studying but are instead 'waiting for God's Word to us'.[8] Interpreters often miss this point. Even the introduction to volume 5 of the English translation of the critical edition (*DBWE 5*) mistakenly states that in *Life Together* we find 'a detailed account of how the day was to be spent in a structured balance of devotions, study, [and] classes . . .'.[9] For sure, we know that Finkenwalde included study and classes. Volume 14 contains a wealth of insight into such things. But *Life Together* doesn't.

This discrepancy between Volume 14 and Volume 5 might suggest that Bonhoeffer intentionally trimmed out the specifically theological dimensions of Finkenwalde in order to make *Life Together* accessible to a broader audience as a manual on how to form spiritual community. Hence the popularity of the first interpretive option. But perhaps we should dig a bit deeper. Consider, for a moment, what Bonhoeffer elsewhere says about the task of studying theology. 'To speak of Christ is to be silent', he suggests.[10] When doing theology we must '[leave] room to the reality of God'.[11] One must 'ton[e] down one's self',[12] and one should 'err on the side of being too quiet rather than too loud'.[13]

Perhaps, therefore, we can imagine that Bonhoeffer's silence in *Life Together* concerning matters of theological education is precisely the point. The book as a whole, with its idiosyncratic prescriptions and its total lack of reflection on education, reads as a concrete depiction of the 'toning down' that constitutes the foundation of the theological task; it reads as a sustained attempt to form a community that leaves room to the reality of God.

---

8. Bonhoeffer, *DBWE* 5, 87.
9. Geffrey B Kelly, 'Editor's Introduction to the English Edition', *DBWE* 5, 14.
10. Bonhoeffer, *DBWE* 12, 300.
11. Bonhoeffer, *DBWE* 10, 455.
12. Bonhoeffer, *DBWE* 12, 433.
13. .. Bonhoeffer, *DBWE* 12, 435.

Life Together as the culmination of Bonhoeffer's theological trajectory

With this interpretation, an intriguing possibility comes into focus. Rather than a spiritual addendum to Bonhoeffer's social and ethical concerns or a historically contingent side project, *Life Together* emerges as the culmination of his theological trajectory. From his student days, he set his mind to think about the nature of authentic God-talk and God-knowledge. He frames *Act and Being*, for instance, as an attempt to sort through the various theological conceptualities on offer in search of a more satisfying alternative.[14] At the beginning of that work he gestures toward his constructive path forward when he claims that 'the concept of revelation must . . . yield an epistemology of its own'.[15] He is suggesting, in other words, that the formation of genuine theological knowledge requires a mode of knowing unique to revelation, indeed one that revelation itself creates. Revelation changes not only *what* we know but *how* we know; not only the *content* of knowledge but the *mode* of knowledge. What I am wondering, and what I will explore in the rest of this paper, is whether this bold theological agenda that emerges early in his career can help us understand what is going on in his Finkenwalde experiment.

To unpack this possibility let's think more carefully about how Bonhoeffer understands theology. In *Act and Being*, he claims that theological knowledge necessarily exists in two different modes—one that is essentially sacred and another that is essentially profane. The first, the sacred, is the miracle of encountering Christ, being pardoned by him, and being torn out of our sinful incurvature by his gracious word.[16] Being a miracle of grace, this knowledge is not actually open to reflection. It is not knowledge in the way we normally use the word. The moment this event becomes a matter of my consciousness, it ceases to be God's word and instead becomes *my intellectual possession of* God's word—in that moment the sacred becomes profane. Framing the matter in this way makes theological knowledge appear impossible. At the end of *Act and Being* Bonhoeffer explicitly refers to it as 'the paradoxical occurrence of revelation without the

---

14. Bonhoeffer, *DBWE* 2.
15. Bonhoeffer, *DBWE* 2, 31.
16. See Bonhoeffer, *DBWE* 2, 126, where Bonhoeffer speaks of this as a 'believing way of knowing'.

reflexive answer of consciousness'.[17] He is inviting us to see that theology in its sacred mode is a matter of knowledge that is, paradoxically, not even ours.

In practice, this paradox can seem paralyzing—what can we actually do with this sacred account of theology? Genuine God-knowledge, Bonhoeffer seems to be saying, so intensely and directly focuses on Jesus, that any attempt to reflect, even for a moment, on the act and content of human knowing jeopardizes our ability to attend to Christ. It is like a theological staring contest—blink, and you're out. Bonhoeffer was well aware of the practical challenges this poses, which is why he insists that theological reflection must also exist in the aftermath of this miraculous event. As reflection on the memory of past happenings, theological knowledge in this mode exists as a natural quantity, it fits within the mind, it is as profane as any other form of human reflection.

So here is my question: does the essence of theology in its sacred mode carry any consequence for the task of theology in its profane mode? When we prepare sermons, when we teach, when we seek doctrinal clarity, when we engage in the mundane task of theology—we are not in heaven but on earth. So does heaven ever touch earth? Does the miracle of God's revelatory word shape the way we busy ourselves with task of teaching, learning, and speaking rightly about God? Does Bonhoeffer's profound depiction of authentic God-knowledge have any meaningful performative outcomes on the ground?

It seems to me that throughout *Act and Being* Bonhoeffer is primarily concerned with the first mode of knowing, with the knowledge of faith that arises neither from act concepts of revelation nor from being concepts of revelation but from the personal presence of Jesus. This seems to be the structural center of his imagination. Indeed, his deepest concerns come to the fore in his doxological conclusion when he points poetically toward the eschatological possibility of the child, toward—and these are the very last words of the books—'the new creation of those born from out of the world's confines into the wideness of heaven, becoming what they were or never were, a creature of God, a child'.[18] Beautiful—but how does this sacred knowledge, this pure orientation, shape the profane everydayness of our thinking?

---

17. Bonhoeffer, *DBWE* 2, 159.
18. Bonhoeffer, *DBWE* 2, 161.

One line in *Act and Being*—and this has always struck me as one of the most interesting lines in the book—hints at an answer: 'Here, not in its *method* of thinking, but rather in the *obedience* of thinking, the scholarly discipline of theology does differ fundamentally from everything profane'.[19] As Bonhoeffer goes on to say, this obedience is characterized by humility. Theology *is* like every other profane form of thinking, *except in this one way*—it emerges from a posture of obedience and humility. He makes sure to remind us that this humility cannot be secured by a method. A method, for him, is nothing but a human tool aimed at knowledge acquisition. It is inherently profane. Method, in and of itself, presses toward hubris, not humility. He thus claims, for example, that even the early Barth's dialectical method, which on the surface seems an eminently humble endeavor, is actually no less profane than any other theological system.[20] No method can secure theology's obedience.

This is why theology has a distinct location. The great danger constantly facing the theologian is that the act of reflection 'turns revelation into something that exists'. For Bonhoeffer, there is one antidote: that we practice theology 'where the living person of Christ . . . can destroy this existing thing or acknowledge it. Therefore, theology must be in immediate reference to preaching.'[21] In other words, the theologian embodies a posture of obedience and humility by living between past and future preaching—reflecting on the miracle that *has* occurred in hopes of preparing the preacher for the miracle that *may* occur. As an aside, it is interesting that in this early form, Bonhoeffer has bridged the academic-pastoral divide. I think this is what he means when he later says he never really believed in the academy. The academy, strictly as the academy, never fit into his framework, even at this early stage. His unique epistemology of revelation requires academic theology to sit in the pews.

To say this differently, the presence of the gathered community constitutes the possibility of theology's obedience. As a point of contrast, Bonhoeffer believes that one of the reasons dialectical theology is forced to take its method so seriously is because it functions individualistically, still beholden to idealist epistemology, even if neg-

---

19. Bonhoeffer, *DBWE* 2, 131, emphasis added.
20. Bonhoeffer, *DBWE* 2, 131.
21. Bonhoeffer, *DBWE* 2, 131.

atively. Whatever dialectical theology has to do with method, Bonhoeffer says we must do with humility and obedience, which means, in community.[22]

So, to repeat that key line: it is not theology's method but rather its obedience that constitutes its difference from all profane modes of knowing. At just this point it becomes appropriate to direct our attention to *Life Together*. It reads, I' am suggesting, as a sustained attempt to shape not the method of thinking but its obedience, the posture of thinking that is fundamental to the task of theology. When the sacred trickles down to the profane, it looks like *Life Together*.

Connections between *Act and Being* and *Life Together*

I wonder, in other words, if we can read *Life Together* as the practical consequence of the epistemology of revelation he unpacks in *Act and Being*.

The connections between the two works are not difficult to notice, but let me draw attention to a few in order to make the point. During his student days he suggests, in dense philosophical terminology, that sin leads to 'ethical atomism',[23] that the *cor curvum in se* represents the 'ontic inversion of the self',[24] and that the all-knowing I does violence to reality by pulling it within the circle of the self.[25] In *Life Together* he makes the same point by claiming that the way between two Christians is blocked by the ego.[26] The enemy of authentic knowledge is also the enemy of authentic community. Indeed, in *Life Together* genuine community breaks forth precisely when the other ceases to be an idea the ego can manipulate and instead becomes a person standing over-against the self.[27] The idiosyncratic distinction Bonhoeffer makes in *Life Together* between community that is emotional (*seelisch*) and spiritual (*geistlich*) seems to reflect this basic insight.

In a similar manner, Bonhoeffer's concern in *Act and Being* about the *extra nos* nature of justification becomes concrete in *Life Together* as the exteriority of other Christians. 'God puts his word in the

---

22. Bonhoeffer, *DBWE* 2, 132.
23. Bonhoeffer, *DBWE* 1, 107.
24. Bonhoeffer, *DBWE* 2, 46.
25. Bonhoeffer, *DBWE* 10, 452.
26. Bonhoeffer, *DBWE* 5, 33.
27. Bonhoeffer, *DBWE* 5, 100.

mouths of human beings so it may be passed on to others', he suggests in the latter work.[28] He is bold enough to suggest that 'the goal of all Christian community is to encounter one another as bringers of the message of salvation'.[29] And he goes *even one step* further: 'Christ made the other Christian to *be* grace for us'.[30] The other is not merely a messenger of grace; the other actually *is* it. This conviction animates his highly prescriptive account of the politics of togetherness. We must attend carefully to the ways we bear the proximity of others and navigate the task of listening and speaking to them, for I encounter the otherness of Christ's grace as I experience the otherness of the community he creates. We need alien bodies to speak an alien word.

In this sense, the person-concept of revelation that emerges in *Act and Being* takes shape in *Life Together* as the 'yearning for the physical presence of other Christians'.[31] If God encounters us through other persons, then how we hash out the mechanics of bodies gathered is a matter of how we situate ourselves to bear Christ's presence. Or to say this differently, near the conclusion of *Act and Being* Bonhoeffer highlights 'Luther's countlessly repeated admonition not to look upon one's own repentance . . . but precisely upon the Lord . . . For . . . as long as I still reflect on myself, Christ is not present'.[32] As noted, there is something beautiful about this, but also something impossible. How do we actually *do* that? Well, *Life Together* puts it nicely: 'We must be ready . . . to be interrupted by God, who will [send] people across our path'.[33] Bonhoeffer is inviting us to see that the way we avoid the constant self-reflection about which Luther warns is to learn to be in community. You cannot focus on yourself when you are focusing on someone else.

As he puts it in his early work, we cannot draw our own boundary. But as he adds in *Life Together*, 'I will respect the other as the

---

28. Bonhoeffer, *DBWE* 5, 32.
29. Bonhoeffer, *DBWE* 5, 32.
30. Bonhoeffer, *DBWE* 5, 109, emphasis added.
31. Bonhoeffer, *DBWE* 5, 29. For Bonhoeffer's earlier account of the "person-concept" of revelation, see *DBWE* 2, 115, 128. The best recent exposition of this theme is Michael DeJonge, *Bonhoeffer's Theological Formation: Berlin, Barth, and Protestant Theology* (Oxford: Oxford University Press, 2012), 56–82.
32. Bonhoeffer, *DBWE* 2, 142.
33. Bonhoeffer, *DBWE* 5, 99.

boundary that Christ establishes between us'.[34] We cannot coerce God to speak. As he suggests to his Finkenwalde students, we can listen before we speak.[35] As he says in *Act and Being*, we cannot on our volition place ourselves in the truth.[36] But as he adds in *Life Together*—we can place ourselves next to someone else. The politics of togetherness—agreeing not talk about another behind their back, intentionally pursuing genuine friendship, going on long walks together, playing games together, eating together, singing together (all things Bonhoeffer required of his students)—that is how this community practiced a form of life that made encounter with God possible.

As one former student put so well, 'It was the peripheral things that enhanced my delight in what was central'.[37] What this student means is that for him, the friendships, the mutual respect, the 'hearty laughter' as he puts it—these things made his education come to life. Bonhoeffer might respond: yes, indeed—but these peripheral things actually are not peripheral at all.

Togetherness as an epistemological program

A glance at Bonhoeffer's famous claim in *Discipleship* may be helpful here: 'Do not interpret or apply but do it and obey. That is the only way Jesus' word is really heard'.[38] Here Bonhoeffer depicts discipleship in epistemological terms, as a condition of truthful knowledge. He continues, 'We have heard the Sermon on the Mount; perhaps we have understood it. But who has heard it correctly?'[39] With this distinction, he opens up a radical idea. Semantic truth—a true statement, a true doctrine, a true interpretation—might actually be false. This is why he distinguishes between knowledge as a conclusion and knowledge as a presupposition and why he thereby insists that 'knowledge cannot be separated from the existence in which it was acquired'.[40]

I am suggesting that *Life Together* depicts an existence through which knowledge may be acquired. It is Bonhoeffer's attempt to

---

34. Bonhoeffer, *DBWE* 5, 44.
35. Bonhoeffer, *DBWE* 5, 98–99.
36. Bonhoeffer, *DBWE* 2, 81.
37. Bonhoeffer, *DBWE* 15, 129.
38. Bonhoeffer, *DBWE* 4, 181.
39. Bonhoeffer, *DBWE* 4, 180.
40. Bonhoeffer, *DBWE* 4, 51.

articulate the conditions for truthful knowledge and speech. It's the process by which theological knowledge becomes a conclusion and not a mere presupposition. Or to put this in terms of his early writings: if revelation must yield an epistemology of its own, *Life Together* sketches this epistemology. It sketches a picture of what revelation looks like in practice.

To put this in an even different idiom, perhaps we can say that togetherness functions for Bonhoeffer as the epistemic condition necessary to discern Jesus.[41] Perhaps togetherness functions, as others have put it, as an "epistemic apparatus" and an 'epistemological program' that the community enacts over time as a means of becoming fit for knowing Christ.[42] On this account, we can say that grace changes our epistemological apparatus by changing the way we manage the proximity of others in community. No wonder Jesus asks his disciples to put down their nets (Matt 4:19–20) before he asks them 'who do you say that I am?' (Matt 16:15). The process of reorienting their bodies in a new community around him was the necessary condition for answering his question. It was how knowledge became possible.

Conclusion

My point, to put it simply, is that *Life Together* sketches in thick terminology how the profane task of theology differs from other profane forms of thinking. It shows us what revelation looks like in practice. Given this interpretation, the silence in *Life Together* concerning matters of formal theological education is one of the book's great strengths, for it exemplifies Bonhoeffer's conviction that knowledge is

---

41. Here I take cues from Sarah Coakley, particularly her work *Powers and Submissions: Spirituality, Gender, and Philosophy* (Malden, MA: Wiley-Blackwell, 2002).

42. Coakley, *Powers and Submissions*, 130–131. Throughout her work Coakley speaks about the literal epistemological transformation necessary to discern Jesus. She speaks of certain "practices of unmastery" that lead to an altered epistemic condition; see Coakley, *Powers and Submissions*, 139. Elsewhere she writes about practices that expand one's ability to respond to Jesus; see *God, Sexuality and the Self: An Essay 'On the Trinity'* (Cambridge: Cambridge University Press, 2013), 26. I am suggesting here that we can use Coakley's terminology as a lens for understanding how community functions epistemologically for Bonhoeffer.

not about ideas but about life. Faithful theology is less about method than about posture. We cannot do with our minds what we can only do with our bodies.

The answer to Bonhoeffer's early epistemological questions is not a theory but a community, which would mean, then, that *Life Together* is the closest we can get in book form to his understanding of the nature of authentic theological knowledge. He cannot directly convey this knowledge through writing, but by describing the contours of this community, in all its profane particularity, he shows us one way it might become possible.

Vol 6 No 1/2018

Bonhoeffer's Criticism of Barth's 'Positivism of Revelation' and its Implications for Natural Theology

Peter Truasheim

Introduction

This article employs a comparative methodology to examine the implications of what Bonhoeffer called Barth's 'positivism of revelation'. The 'positivism of revelation' can be understood as a revelation which is limited to the Word found in the scriptures, and its interpretation within the sphere of the church. Hence, Barth's, Bonhoeffer's and Brunner's theologies on the subject of revelation are compared. Also, some parallels to work found in the documents of the Second Vatican Council and statements by Pope Francis are noted. This is not intended to be an argument in support of neo-reformation theology so much as evidence for the compatibility between Bonhoeffer and contemporary Catholicism.

First, the context for the 'positivism of revelation' will be discussed in order to provide a background as to why Barth's theology developed into what Bonhoeffer called a 'positivism of revelation'. After discussing the what and the why of the 'positivism of revelation', the essay examines Bonhoeffer's Christology, which is then followed by an exploration of the foundations for a Christian natural theology. This examination will help clarify the reason for the different interpretations of natural revelation by Barth, Brunner and Bonhoeffer. Once these theologians' concepts of natural theology have been compared, the subjects of how the transcendent Christ passes on revelation and how reality came into being during creation are discussed. Finally, an interpretation is made of Bonhoeffer's natural and sacramental theology of 'being there for others'. The conclusion considers the challenges artificial intelligence (AI), extremism and authoritarian regimes pose to contemporary societies and how these challenges create a need for a broader view of revelation and an inclusive natural and sacramental theology in what Bonhoeffer called 'the world come of age'.

The context for the Positivism of Revelation

Barth, Bonhoeffer and Brunner were influenced by the liberal the-ology of their time. Liberal theology developed when the historical critical method and literary criticism attempted to establish a histori-cal Jesus based more on fact and less on belief.[1] Barth, Bonhoeffer and Brunner moved away from liberal theology to neo-reformation the-ology, also known as neo-orthodoxy. Their goal was to return to the origins of Christianity.[2] This new direction was partially motivated by a desire to restore a Christian conscience to the German people and churches at a time when Hitler's Nazi party attempted to usurp the human conscience with a state conscience.[3]

Barth's work, *The Epistle to the Romans,* provoked much thought during the development of neo-reformation theology. The basis of his ideas can be seen in the following quote: 'The Gospel is not a religious message . . . The Gospel is the Word of the Primal origin of all things.'[4] This 'Primal origin' bears some similarity to Bonhoeffer's concept of 'religionless Christianity', in its reference to a primordial belief that pre-dates and superordinates religion in general and organisational Christianity as an instance.[5] Similarly, Brunner differentiated between the organisational and the primordial/religionless by separating the church into two categories, the 'historical institution' and the '*ecclesia*'.[6]

Barth and the Positivism of Revelation: The what and the why?

The unity that Barth, Bonhoeffer and Brunner enjoyed in neo-ref-ormation theology did not mean there were no differences between

1. Bonhoeffer, *DBWE* 12, 328; Mark Wallace, 'Karl Barth's Hermeneutic: A Way Beyond Impasse', in *The Journal of Religion* 68/3 (1988): 396–410.
2. Nicholas Healy, 'Neo-Reformation theology', in *The Routledge Companion to the Christian Church*, edited by Lewis Mudge and Gerard Mannion (Hoboken: Routledge, 2007), 114–115; Henry Carrigan Jr, 'Emil Brunner (1889–1966)', in *The Encyclopaedia of Christian Literature*, edited by George Kurin and James Smith (Plymouth: Scarecrow Press, 2010), 226.
3. John Moses, 'Bonhoeffer and the Powers-that-Be', in *Pacifica* 25/2 (2012): 132–133.
4. Karl Barth, *The Epistle to the Romans*, sixth edition, translated by Edwyn Hoskyns (London: Oxford University Press, 1968), 28.
5. 5 Bonhoeffer, *DBWE* 8, 363.
6. Emil Brunner, *The Misunderstanding of the Church* (Cambridge: Lutterworth Press, 1952), 15–17.

them. Brunner advocated an opaque natural theology that Barth strongly opposed while Bonhoeffer criticised Barth for his 'positivism of revelation'.[7] Barth's 'positivism of revelation' made scripture the only source wherein revelation could be found in an uncorrupted form, so he proposed that the revelation recorded in scripture should be protected by a 'law of faith'.[8]

In the following quote, Bonhoeffer explains some of the shortcomings of what he calls Barth's 'positivism of revelation':

> Barth was the first theologian—to his great and lasting credit—to begin the critique of religion, but he then put in its place a positivist doctrine of revelation that says, in effect, 'like it or lump it'. Whether it's the virgin birth, the Trinity, or anything else, all are equally significant and necessary parts of the whole, which must be swallowed whole or not at all. That's not biblical. There are degrees of cognition and degrees of significance. That means an "arcane discipline" must be re-established, through which the mysteries of the Christian faith are sheltered against profanation. The positivism of revelation is too easy-going, since in the end it sets up a law of faith and tears up what is—through Christ's becoming flesh!—a gift for us.[9]

In the quote above, Bonhoeffer criticises Barth for starting but not completing his journey towards a religionless Christianity, or 'arcane discipline' which Barth described as: 'the Word of the Primal origin of all things'.[10] Bonhoeffer argues that Barth liberated revelation from the distortion that the liberalism of their time placed upon it, returning it to an orthodoxy of scripture within the Christian churches.

---

7. More information on the 'positivism of revelation' and the interactions between Barth and Bonhoeffer can be found in the following publications: Matthew Puffer, 'Dietrich Bonhoeffer in the Theology of Karl Barth,' in *Karl Barth in Conversation*, edited by Travis McMaken and David Congdon (Eugene: Pickwick, 2004), 46–62; Andreas Pangritz, *Karl Barth in the Theology of Dietrich Bonhoeffer* (Michigan: Eerdmans, 2000), 71–86, 143–145.

8. Bonhoeffer, *DBWE* 8, 373; Charles Marsh, *Reclaiming Dietrich Bonhoeffer: The Promise of His Theology* (Oxford: Oxford University Press, 1994), 20; Rodney Holder, *The Heavens Declare: Natural Theology and the Legacy of Karl Barth* (West Conshohocken: Templeton Press, 2012), 90–91.

9. Bonhoeffer, *DBWE* 8, 373.

10. Barth, *Romans*, 28.

However, according to Bonhoeffer, Barth fell short of reaching the primordial origin of revelation which comes from the transcendent Word of God who became flesh in the person of Jesus Christ. The revelation of the primordial Word of God, which was not confined to scripture, and could not possibly have been because the canon of the Bible had not yet been determined and decided upon, was and is given to people of faith, such as Noah, Abraham, and others, including those mentioned in Hebrews chapter 11. However, Bonhoeffer asserts that Barth placed limits on a limitless God by restricting revelation to scripture as determined by the Christian churches only. Bonhoeffer considered this to be a process designed to '[set] up a law of faith and [tear] up what is—through Christ's becoming flesh!—a gift for us.' This law of faith also creates a scenario for contention and division because Christian churches can compete for the authority to interpret accurately the scriptures. Also, it excludes those of other religions because of their lack of access to the Holy Scriptures. The Second Vatican Council also made an effort to move away from the exclusiveness of religion or 'positivism of revelation' by acknowledging the primordiality of God. The following quote from explains the power of the primordial God to affect people's consciousness throughout time:

> From ancient times down to the present, there is found among various peoples a certain perception of that hidden power which hovers over the course of things and over the events of human history; at times some indeed have come to the recognition of a Supreme Being, or even of a Father. This perception and recognition penetrates their lives with a profound religious sense.[11]

In the following quote, written in prison, Bonhoeffer envisions a religionlessness unencumbered by the 'positivism of revelation'. The 'religionless Christianity' mentioned in this quote is what Bonhoeffer argues could be the answer to reaching people with the gospel in what he envisioned could be the predominantly secular or 'religionless world' of the future:

---

11. Paul VI, *Nostra Aetate: Declaration on the Relation of the Church to Non-Christian Religions* (1965). http://www.vatican.va/archive/hist_councils/ii_vatican_council/documents/vat-ii_decl_19651028_nostra-aetate_en.htmlparagraph 2.

How can Christ become Lord of the religionless as well? Is there such a thing as a religionless Christian? If religion is only the garb in which Christianity is clothed—and this garb has looked very different in different ages—what then is religionless Christianity? Barth, who is the only one to have begun thinking along these lines, nevertheless did not pursue these thoughts all the way, did not think them through, but ended up with a positivism of revelation, which in the end essentially remained a restoration. For the working person or any person who is without religion, nothing decisive has been gained here. The questions to be answered would be: What does a church, a congregation, a sermon, a liturgy, a Christian life, mean in a religionless world? How do we talk about God—without religion, that is, without the temporally conditioned presuppositions of metaphysics, the inner life, and so on? How do we speak (or perhaps we can no longer even 'speak' the way we used to) in a 'worldly' way about 'God'? How do we go about being 'religionless-worldly' Christians, how can we be ἐκ-κλησία [ecclesia], those who are called out, without understanding ourselves religiously as privileged, but instead seeing ourselves as belonging wholly to the world? Christ would then no longer be the object of religion, but something else entirely, truly lord of the world. But what does that mean? In a religionless situation, what do ritual [Kultus] and prayer mean? Is this where the 'arcane discipline' [Arkandisziplin], or the difference (which you've heard about from me before) between the penultimate and the ultimate, have new significance?[12]

Bonhoeffer's Christology

The topics of 'religionless Christianity', 'Primordial origin' and the transcendent and physical 'Word of God' can be informed by an examination of Bonhoeffer's Christology found in his university lectures from 1932 to 1933.[13] This in turn can provide a context for his critique of Barth's positivism.

---

12. Bonhoeffer, *DBWE* 8, 363–365.
13. Bonhoeffer, *DBWE* 12.

Bonhoeffer understood Jesus Christ to be the human form of the Word of God, the source of revelation. He explains: 'God's revelation . . . takes place through the Word.'[14] He also called Christ the Logos of God. In this context, he associated Logos with knowledge, so he understood the Logos to be God's knowledge. 'It is knowledge par excellence. From outside, Christology becomes the center of knowledge. The Logos we are talking about here is a person. This human person is the transcendent.'[15] Here we see revelation happening through the eternal Christ (the transcendent) and also in the person of Jesus Christ. 'Christology, with its claim to be the center of the sphere of knowledge, stands alone. It cannot point to anything other than the transcendence of its object.'[16] Later, in *Letters and Papers from Prison*, Bonhoeffer explains that a transcendent relationship with Christ is found through 'being there for others'.[17]

The foundations for a Christian natural theology

Christian natural theology is another topic that helps to provide further context to the debate between Barth, Brunner and Bonhoeffer. These theologians each had a different interpretation about the part that natural theology can play in the revelation of God's Word. While natural theology rests on the view that traces of God are revealed in the natural world, it is also, for Christians, implicitly connected to Christology because the Incarnation is about God's presence among us in Jesus Christ. The Gospel of John says: 'And the Word became flesh and lived among us' (Jn 1:14 NRSV). Here we see the Word of God becoming a human being in order to restore humanity and nature to their original perfection (Coloss 1:15). However, even before Christ's Incarnation, according to scripture, there was some limited communication of God's Word through nature. The following verses are examples of this: 'Ever since the creation of the world his eternal power and divine nature, invisible though they are, have been understood and seen through the things he has made' (Rom 1:20).

---

14. Bonhoeffer, *DBWE* 12, 300.
15. Bonhoeffer, *DBWE* 12, 301.
16. Bonhoeffer *DBWE* 12, 301.
17. Bonhoeffer *DBWE* 8, 501.

The Hebrew Bible also acknowledges that nature speaks to us: 'The heavens are telling the glory of God' (Ps 19:1).

Jesus offered a strong endorsement of such a natural theology in the following verse: 'I tell you, if these were silent, the stones would shout out' (Lk 19:40). This would indicate that there is an imperative in nature to reveal God's Word. In the following quote, Barth also acknowledges that there is a force pushing us towards God: 'Nevertheless, it is, in fact, always God against whom we are thrust. Even the unbeliever encounters God, but does not penetrate through to the truth of God that is hidden from him.'[18]

Paul also speaks of a dark side to natural theology. This darkness is a kind of corruption which hinders nature from speaking clearly. In the following verse, Paul explains this lack of clarity.

> For now we see in a mirror, dimly, but then we will see face to face. Now I know only in part; then I will know fully, even as I have been fully known. (1 Corinthians 13:12)

In the last part of this verse, Paul explains that there will be a time when revelation will be completely clear and known. In Romans, Paul also refers to how 'sin came into the world through one man' (Rom 5:12). Here, he speaks to the story in Genesis in which Adam and Eve were deceived by falsity (Gen 3:1–7). The birth, death and resurrection of Jesus Christ play a crucial part in the restoration of creation to its original perfection (Rom 5:12–21; Romans 15:12–19).

> And through him God was pleased to reconcile to himself all things, whether on earth or in heaven, by making peace through the blood of his cross. (Colossians 1:20)

In the following quote, Paul indicates that this process of redemption has already started:

> We know that the whole creation has been groaning in labor pains until now; and not only the creation, but we ourselves, who have the first fruits of the Spirit, groan inwardly while we wait for adoption, the redemption of our bodies. (Romans 8:22-23)

---

18. Barth, *Romans*, 43.

Also, the Book of Isaiah talks about a time when the 'knowledge of the Lord' will be universally known and nature and humanity will live in peace and harmony (Isa11:6–8).

There are some differences, however, in how Bonhoeffer, Barth and Brunner each interpreted the role of natural theology. The following sections examine the tensions between these three theologians regarding the extent to which natural theology plays a meaningful role in ascertaining revelation. Barth wished to restrict revelation to scripture within the sphere of the church, while Brunner believed an opaque revelation through nature was possible.[19] Bonhoeffer, however, believed that nature sometimes played a part in revelation while, at other times, it was unable to speak to it.[20] Some insight can be gained by comparing the arguments that underpin their central theologies.

Barth's interpretation of Natural Theology

Barth's approach can be described as being like that of a fundamentalist because he wished to protect and restrict revelation with a 'law of faith'.[21] Most likely, this was because he experienced the church being compromised during the Nazification of Germany. Barth's 'positivism of revelation', in part, was motivated by a desire to protect the world and Christianity from a reoccurrence of those events.[22] Jürgen Moltmann, when talking about Barth in an interview with Tony Jones at the 2009 Emergent Village Theological Conversation, explained that, in his opinion, Barth's denial of natural theology was a result of the German Christians' misplaced belief in the concept of the 'blood and soil of the German Race, and the Germanic historic figure of the victorious Christ'.[23] Barth was concerned that the doctrines of 'blood

---

19. Bonhoeffer, *DBWE* 8, 373; Marsh, *Reclaiming Dietrich Bonhoeffer,* 20; Rodney Holder, *The Heavens Declare*, 29, 90–91.
20. Bonhoeffer, *DBWE* 12, 327.
21. Bonhoeffer, *DBWE* 8, 373.
22. Bonhoeffer, *DBWE* 8, 373; Woodard-Lehman and Derek Alan, 'Reason After Revelation: Karl Barth on Divine Word and Human Words', in *Modern Theology* 33/1 (2017): 97, 115.
23. Jürgen Moltmann and Tony Jones, *PostBarthian: Jürgen Moltmann at the Emergent Village Theological Conversation in 2009* (audio), part 2, 15:15–15:29. https://postbarthian.com/2014/07/14/jurgen-moltmann-emergent-village-theological-conversation-2009/ (accessed July 17, 2019).

and soil' and the 'victorious Christ' were given licence by natural theology. This concern may have caused him to react negatively to Brunner's acknowledgment of an opaque natural theology to which Barth gave an emphatic '*nein!*'[24]

Barth nonetheless acknowledged a form of natural theology. In the following quote, he is seen to be talking about a revelation through nature which is hidden by 'arrogance', one that 'encased the truth of God and evoked His wrath':

> And so through all history there runs the line of intersection between time and eternity, between the present and the future world. Long ago it was proclaimed; always it was visible . . . for the clearly seen works of God speak of His everlasting power . . . Inexcusable is their unrighteousness, for the clearly seen facts bear witness to the everlasting divinity of God, and have already risen up in protest against the arrogance of religion, by which men, speaking of God from the welter of their experiences, mean in fact themselves. We have, therefore, encased the truth of God and evoked His wrath.[25]

Moltmann also found Barth's natural theology argument to be somewhat contradictory as he seemed to change his position from the 'No!' given to Brunner to his own acknowledgment of a natural theology at the end of his *Church Dogmatics* thirty years later. Moltmann explains this in the following:

> This is against Karl Barth of course, because in 1933–4, he struggled with . . . Emil Brunner on Natural Theology. [Barth argued] there must be no Natural Theology, only the self-revelation of God. This was not the problem of a theology of nature, it was the problem of political theology of the German Christians, who believe instead of the Old Testament, in blood and soil of the German Race, and the Germanic heroic figure of a victorious Christ, etcetera, etcetera. So, to [correct] the German Christians, [Barth] said there must be no Natural Theology. While at the end of his Church Dogmatics, he developed his own Natural Theology. [Barth argued that]

---

24. Rodney Holder, *The Heavens Declare: Natural Theology and the Legacy of Karl Barth* (West Conshohocken, PA: Templeton Press, 2012), 29–30.

25. Barth, *Romans*, 47.

after the special Christian Theology, there can and must be a theology of nature about the many lights outside of the one light of Christ, and the many words of truth outside of the One Word of the Incarnate of God, which is Christ. But the relationship between the Light which is Christ and the many lights in the world, is like the headlights of your car. If you switch on the lights of your car, then you can see the reflectors [behind the light], so the lights in nature are only a reflection of the Light of Christ. They do not illuminate anything by themselves; only as a reflection of the Light of Christ. When Emil Brunner . . . read this volume of the Church Dogmatics, [he] was curious, because he had said the same thing thirty years ago and Karl Barth then came to the same result, that Natural Theology or Theology of Nature, is a task of Christian Theology. We are not only an ideology for insiders . . . not only a theology for Christians. We have a theology for the Kingdom of God, for the mission of those who are outside. I remember there was a similar struggle between the Yale school and the Chicago school. While the Yale school followed Karl Barth that Christian Theology is only for Christians. The Chicago school said, no, it's for everyone who can listen, because otherwise there can be no real mission. And I think from my standpoint theology is a theology of the Kingdom of God which is coming. So, we have a special starting point which is Jesus Christ and the experience of the Holy Spirit and a universal horizon which we can discover in the New Testament and the letters of the Apostle Paul, Colossians and everywhere. So, God reconciled the whole cosmos to himself, and made us messengers of the reconciliation. We need this universal horizon if we are to be faithful to the gospel. But there is in Karl Barth, also this type of hidden Universalism. Not to reconcile the universe but to reconcile everybody.[26]

Brunner's interpretation of Natural Theology

Emil Brunner was more of an idealist compared to Barth because of his commitment to the ideals of the ecumenical movement which aimed to unite Christianity and create dialogue. He argued that there is an opaque form of natural theology. This interpretation of natu-

---

26. Jürgen Moltmann and Tony Jones, *PostBarthian*, part 2, 14:40–19:25.

ral theology can assist the ecumenical movement because it allows for more flexibility and inclusiveness within Christianity.[27] Brunner's book, *The Misunderstanding of the Church,* described the church as the *ecclesia*, the body of believers. This was an inclusive concept which promoted dialogue between believers and contributed to the ecumenical movement by giving Christians a common foundation and goal. Brunner was committed to the ecumenical movement and he contributed to the establishment of the World Council of Churches. Carrigan thus comments about Brunner:

> Brunner was passionately committed to the ecumenical movement from 1930 until the end of his life, and his ecumenism grew out of his lifelong commitment to missionary service.'[28]

An argument can be made that Brunner is following Paul's theology, which states: 'For now we see in a mirror, dimly' (1 Cor 13:12a). While Barth espoused the dangers of the brokenness of the Image of God in humanity, Brunner argued that humanity still had a remnant of the Image of God. He called the original image 'material' and the image after the Fall as 'formal', indicating that a Godly morality remained in the human conscience after the Fall. Sudduth describes Brunner's concept in the following way:

> Human persons are sinners, but they are still responsible agents. This responsibility, in as much as it implies conscience, implies some residual knowledge of divine law and knowledge of God. For Brunner, this is a necessary point of contact between God and humans.[29]

Regarding natural theology, Pope Francis also seems to have a similar understanding to that of Brunner. This can be seen by the use of the word 'glimpse' in the following quote from *Laudato Si'*:

27. Carrigan Jr, 'Emil Brunner (1889–1966)', 226.
28. Carrigan Jr, 'Emil Brunner (1889–1966)', 226.
29. Michael Sudduth, *The Reformed Objection to Natural Theology* (Burlington: Ashgate), 122.

> Saint Francis, faithful to Scripture, invites us to see nature as a magnificent book in which God speaks to us and grants us a glimpse of his infinite beauty and goodness.[30]

Bonhoeffer's interpretation of Natural Theology

Bonhoeffer can be described as a visionary because his focus was as much on the future of revelation as on its past. During his early lectures in university, he taught that a revelation through nature was possible through the redemptive power of the elements in the sacraments. He also taught that without this redemption, nature could not speak. This creates a tension in which sometimes nature does speak the Word of God and sometimes it does not.[31]

The connection between Bonhoeffer's natural theology and his sacramental theology is explored in more detail below. However, to gain a deeper understanding of revelation, before exploring this connection, the following section will consider how Bonhoeffer understood the spatial and temporal context in which revelation takes place. His concept of revelation was not confined to a linear timeline of past, present and future.[32]

Passing on Revelation

In Christianity, scripture is considered the authoritative record or revelation. However, many controversies come into being through the different interpretations of scripture. Bonhoeffer and Barth did not confine scripture to a legalistic or literalistic interpretation which applied to everybody, in every place for every time. They argued that revelation came from the eternal Christ who transcends space and time. In the following quote, Bonhoeffer explains his spatial and temporal concept of revelation:

> Christ as Word of God in the sense of word spoken to us does not mean Christ as timeless truth, but rather as truth breaking into a concrete moment, as God's speaking to us. Thus Christ

---

30. Francis, *Laudato Si': On Care For Our Common Home* (Vatican, 24 May 2015): paragraph 12, http://w2.vatican.va/content/francesco/en/encyclicals/documents/papa-francesco_20150524_enciclica-laudato-si.html.
31. Bonhoeffer, *DBWE* 12, 318–323; Marsh, *Reclaiming Dietrich Bonhoeffer*, 26.
32. Bonhoeffer, *DBWE* 12, 300–301.

is not timelessly and universally accessible as an idea; instead, he is heard as Word only there where he allows himself to be heard.[33]

This quote explains that interpretation, or 'truth breaking into a concrete moment', creates a situation in which the eternal Word of God speaks specifically to the believer's time and culture. This 'truth breaking into a concrete moment' may be what James is referring to when he writes about 'the wisdom from above'.[34] Also, this implies that some scriptures do not necessarily have a universal interpretation for all times and cultures. There could be times when a scriptural precedent might not be applicable in a contemporary situation. In this case, God does not allow himself to be heard. As the Second Vatican Council proffered:

> The Holy Spirit must precede and assist, moving the heart and turning it to God, opening the eyes of the mind.[35]

The Word from above is transcendent, in the sense that it is not confined by a traditional concept of time and space. Bonhoeffer explains:

> The Word of God cuts vertically through human words. He said it in Jesus Christ and God speaks this Word anew, again and again, and it should be seized anew, again and again, in faith. It is not a word of continuity, but one descending vertically from above.[36]

Bible and Creation

An understanding of how reality comes into being can also be helpful before discussing Bonhoeffer's sacramental theology. According to the Bible, the Word of God was the mysterious force which brought creation into being. This can be seen in Genesis 1. Here, the words

---

33. Bonhoeffer, *DBWE* 12, 317.
34. Bonhoeffer, *DBWE* 12, 192; Marsh, *Reclaiming Dietrich Bonhoeffer*, 27.
35. Paul VI, *Dei verbum*, the Second Vatican Council's Dogmatic Constitution on Divine Revelation, 1965. http://www.vatican.va/archive/hist_councils/ ii_vatican_council/documents/vat-ii_const_19651118_dei-verbum_en.html, paragraph 5.
36. Bonhoeffer, *DBWE* 12, 192.

'God said' and 'let there be' come before every act of creation. The first example can be found in Genesis 1:3: 'Then God said, "Let there be light"; and there was light'. The act of God's Word bringing creation into being is repeated in verses 6, 9, 11, 14, 20, 22, 26 and 28. The power of the Word to create reality is also stated clearly in John: 'In the beginning was the Word, (Jn 1:1) [and] . . . All things came into being through him' (Jn 1:3). The Second Vatican Council also explains this in the document, *Dei Verbum*:

> God, who through the Word creates all things (see Jn 1:3) and keeps them in existence, gives men an enduring witness to Himself in created realities (see Rom. 1:19–20).[37]

By using virtual reality as an analogy, many similarities can be found between the use of language to create reality in Genesis and a digital reality which is created from human words or computer language in the form of coding. If God uses language to create reality it would be logical to assume, if human beings are made in God's image (Gen 1:26), they would also use language to create realities.

Being there for others: Bonhoeffer's Sacramental Theology

The concepts of reality being formed by the Word and the Word as revelation from above, or in other words the transcendent Word of God, lay the foundation for Bonhoeffer's sacramental theology. Bonhoeffer explained how this sacramental process takes place:

> Sacrament exists only where God, in the midst of the world of creatures, names an element, speaks to it, and hallows it with the particular word God has for it by giving it its name. Through God's speaking to it, this element becomes what it is. This is what happens in the Lord's Supper.[38]

Here, we see in the sacrament, God's conscious observation and the power of his Word transforming nature to return to its original per-

---

37. Paul VI, *Dei verbum*, the Second Vatican Council's Dogmatic Constitution on Divine Revelation, 1965. http://www.vatican.va/archive/hist_councils/ii_vatican_council/documents/vat-ii_const_19651118_dei-verbum_en.html, paragraph 3.
38. Bonhoeffer, *DBWE* 12, 319.

fection. This is the same process which took place during creation. Bonhoeffer also explained that: 'The sacrament is Word of God, for it proclaims the gospel, not as a wordless action, but as action that is made holy and given its meaning by the Word.'[39] In the following quote he also saw how this applied to nature: 'The sacrament, in the form of nature, engages human beings in their nature.'[40] However, he states that not all nature can do this because nature has lost its transparency. An argument can be made that for nature to become revelatory again it needs 'redemption' in order to be 'the sacrament, in the form of nature'.[41]

These quotes indicate Bonhoeffer understood that redemption is linked to a sacramental act. Such a sacramental act can be seen when Jesus gave His life for others (Jn 15:13). Jesus also explains that this sacramental act happens when nature creates new life (Jn 12:24). Bonhoeffer explains in the following quote how the process of creating the original reality at creation is similar to the process of creating the new redeemed reality through the sacrament. 'The God-human Jesus Christ is wholly present in the sacrament. As God spoke at the creation, "'Let there be light'; and there was light", so the Word addressed to the sacrament becomes [reality].'[42] Here, we see how Bonhoeffer determines the conditions by which nature can reveal God's Word and how, sometimes, this revelation is distorted if it is not sacramental. Later, in 'Outline for a Book',[43] Bonhoeffer explains how, even in the church organisation, there can be a distortion of revelation and that Jesus' presence is found by 'being there for others':

> Our relationship to God is no 'religious' relationship to some highest, most powerful, and best Being imaginable—that is no genuine transcendence. Instead, our relation to God is a new life in "being there for others," through participation in the being of Jesus. The transcendent is not the infinite, unattainable tasks, but the neighbour within reach in any given situation. God in human form![44]

---

39. Bonhoeffer, *DBWE* 12, 318.
40. Bonhoeffer, *DBWE* 12, 318.
41. Bonhoeffer, *DBWE* 12, 318.
42. Bonhoeffer, *DBWE* 12, 319.
43. Bonhoeffer, *DBWE* 8, 499.
44. Bonhoeffer, *DBWE* 8, 501.

The Second Vatican Council also explains how revelation is found in an 'inner unity' which happens through the interaction between 'deeds' and 'words'.[45] These deeds are sacrificial and Christ-like acts of love. These acts create a transcendence in which the presence of Jesus is experienced through being there for others. In this process, the person sacrificing becomes united with the presence of Christ through their Christ-like giving, while the person who receives, also becomes united with the presence of Christ because: 'just as you did it to one of the least of these who are members of my family, you did it to me' (Matt 25:40). This presence is found through a Christ-like sacrificial interaction which happens through giving and receiving. The opposite would be an earthly domination and subjection of the weak. The powerful forcing their will on the weak and exploiting them would be a case of nature's revelation being distorted. If this is true of human interactions, it would also be logical to assume that the forces of the natural world would also experience the presence of Christ when they have a redemptive and life-giving interaction, such as when 'a grain of wheat falls into the earth and dies . . . it bears much fruit' (John 12:24). The Book of James refers to these loving and sacrificial occurrences as the wisdom from above and the selfish and subjugating occurrences as the wisdom from below (Jam 3:13–18).

Conclusion

The violent and destructive influences of nationalism and religion, when they are taken to an extreme, are once again becoming more prominent and evident through acts of exclusiveness and cruel domination in the world today. In some countries, totalitarian and one-party governments are taking the place of the people's conscience and replacing it with a state conscience. This weakening of the human conscience is potentially being further enabled by the introduction of Artificial Intelligence (AI), machine generated learning and the introduction of social credit rankings which are being determined by algorithms. The pervasiveness of AI decision-making and its lack of

---

45. Paul VI, *Dei verbum*, the Second Vatican Council's Dogmatic Constitution on Divine Revelation, 1965. http://www.vatican.va/archive/hist_councils/ ii_vatican_council/documents/vat-ii_const_19651118_dei-verbum_en.html, paragraph 2.

human oversight is also becoming pervasive in democratic nations as well as authoritarian ones. These new trends need to be kept in their proper place with checks and balances to avoid the mistakes of the past. The following is an example of when such a mistake was made:

> Bonhoeffer was appalled by the Nazi doctrine that the individual had to surrender his or her conscience to the Führer. This would be unconditionally abandoning one's will or individual autonomy to an alien agency, that is, allowing one's will to be determined by something other than the moral law. For a Christian to do this would be like substituting Hitler as the person to whom one seeks personal integrity for Christ. So, to allocate to the man Hitler the function of one's redeemer would be to submit to the most devastating contradiction to Christian truth.[46]

Current trends which tend to take away the individual's conscience and power to make Godly decisions should be a concern for everybody. These trends need to be countered by restoring human oversight and conscience to institutional systems as well as the right for individuals to exercise their Godly conscience. One way a human heart can be restored in the secular or 'world come of age' would be by promoting Bonhoeffer's concept of 'being there for others'. Acknowledging natural theology—'nature as a magnificent book in which God speaks to us and grants us a glimpse of his infinite beauty and goodness'[47]—is also another way those of various denominations, religions and the non-religious can have constructive and inclusive conversations. The combination of enlightenment through natural theology and sacramental acts of 'being there for others' allows all humanity to experience the transcendent Christ and become a part of bringing the Kingdom of God on Earth in the 'world come of age'.

---

46. Pangritz, 'Dietrich Bonhoeffer's *Begriindung*,' 505, cited in John Moses, 'Bonhoeffer and the Powers-that Be,' 132–133.
47. Francis, *Laudato Si': On Care For Our Common Home*. (Vatican, 24 May 2015): paragraph 12, http://w2.vatican.va/content/francesco/en/encyclicals/documents/papa-francesco_20150524_enciclica-laudato-si.html, paragraph 12.

Vol 6 No 1/2018

Book Review
The Cross of Reality: Luther's *Theologia Crucis* and Bonhoeffer's Christology

by H Gaylon Barker (Minneapolis: Fortress Press, 2015).

ISBN: 978-1-4514-8880-7 (A$58) (480 pages)

I first met H Gaylon Barker when he was President of the International Bonhoeffer Society, English Language Division, and was immediately struck by his pastoral concern for people, including his generous welcome to me into that community. As a Bonhoeffer scholar, Barker represents that era of academics, now well known to us, who took Bonhoeffer's work and articulated it for a broader audience. In Barker's case, he co-edited volume 14 of *DBWE* (*Theological Education at Finkenwalde: 1935–1937*) as well as serving on the editorial board of the series. His credentials are well-established, along with his long teaching career, and his reworked doctoral thesis demonstrates a long and careful consideration of the material. But it is Barker's interest in people that characterises his application of Bonhoeffer's theology. Barker pastors St Andrew's Lutheran Church, Ridgefield, Connecticut and his ability to communicate the heart of Bonhoeffer's material has been refined in the context of his pastoral ministry.

Barker's project traces the use and influence of Luther's *theologia crucis* in Bonhoeffer's own theology. For this reason, alone, it is a useful textbook for seminary students. However, Barker has written a book that captures the spirit of Bonhoeffer's own quest to discover and implement an appropriate Christianity for the contemporary age and as such is recommended reading for a broad audience. He traces the development of Bonhoeffer's Christology through his academic and church careers, always contextualising the theology with Bonhoeffer's biography, contemporaneously asking how we might consider these questions in our own time. Throughout, he demonstrates that a God so interested in the world is never far from it but rather, is intimately connected to it through Christ. He writes that Bonhoeffer expressed his thinking through his questions, questions of faith:

1. In 1928 Barcelona, the question was, 'What does the cross have to say to us, today?'
2. A few years later in *Discipleship*, the question was stated in terms of responsibility: 'What does Jesus Christ want of us?'
3. When writing to his seminarians in 1939, it became a question of the proclamation of the gospel to a troubled world: 'We are preachers of justification through grace alone. What [does] that mean today?'
4. Finally, *in Letters and Papers from Prison*, it became, 'What is Christianity or who is Christ actually for us today?'

> Each question is an attempt to answer the same basic question from different perspectives. And always the answer points to the cross. And what is revealed there is God not in transcendent eternity but God for us.[1]

Barker manages to portray the deep connection of the theology of the cross to the everyday life of the Christian disciple. For Barker, Bonhoeffer's theology necessarily requires a response to the God who is 'for us'. That response is in a type of discipleship that must come to terms with Christ who is adamantly for the world, and it manifests in the type of church-communities we create. Barker reminds the church of the centrality of the *theologia crucis* to the Christian faith, that everything we know of God is through Christ and the key to understanding Christ is through the cross. Where Barker sees Bonhoeffer's progression from Luther is primarily in Bonhoeffer's ongoing quest for contextuality. Barker urges us to ask, with Bonhoeffer, who Christ is for us and the world today, and how might our church-communities best reflect that. The cross of reality demands our utmost attention to the needs of the world, and I would add, the needs of Earth herself. Barker's *The Cross of Reality* is highly recommended as a comprehensive but accessible purview of Bonhoeffer's Christology and an encouragement to the church-community and its pastors.

Dianne Rayson
The University of Newcastle, Australia

---

1. H. Gaylon Barker, *The Cross of Reality: Luther's Theologia Crucis and Bonhoeffer's Christology* (Minneapolis: Fortress Press, 2015), 418.

Music Review
Silent Voices by Sunshine Cleaners

The album titled *Silent Voices* by the group, Sunshine Cleaners, constitutes ten songs inspired by Dietrich Bonhoeffer's Prison Poems. The group is comprised of Sjef Herman, Jacqueline Heijmans and Geert de Heer, three Dutch musicians who have taken elements of Bonhoeffer's poetry and put them to musical scores. The result is an appropriately simple yet alluring means of eliciting the spirit of Bonhoeffer's reflections, many of them concerning death, eternal life and personal legacy, in a unique and highly creative way. The melodies and vocals fit well the sentiments of his prison theology as Bonhoeffer scholars have come to understand them. Amidst the many innovative ways in which Bonhoeffer inspires imaginative thought and creative practice, this album is worthy of a place. It represents a contribution in its own way to the legacy to which this journal is dedicated.

Sjef Hermans, the songs' writer, can be contacted at thebigchief37@gmail.com

Terence Lovat
The University of Newcastle, Australia

Contributors

Rev'd Dr Keith Clements is one of the foremost Bonhoeffer scholars in the world today. He is a former General Secretary of The Conference of European Churches and lectured for many years at Bristol Baptist College, UK. He is, among many other things, a member of the Centre for Research in Religion and Social Policy (RASP), University of Divinity, Melbourne, Australia.

Dr Dianne Rayson completed her PhD on Bonhoeffer and Anthropogenic Climate Change in 2017. She currently lectures at The University of Newcastle, Australia and BBI-The Australian Institute of Theological Education, Sydney and is a member of RASP. She is a board member of the International Bonhoeffer Society and a regular presenter at international Bonhoeffer conferences.

Rev'd Professor Dr John Moses is one of Australia's most respected Bonhoeffer scholars. He is an Emeritus of St Mark's College, Charles Sturt University, Canberra, Australia. He has been a regular presenter at international Bonhoeffer conferences over many years.

Dr Derek W Taylor is Director of the Emmaus Scholars Program and a Lecturer in Theology at Whitworth University in Spokane, Washington, USA. His forthcoming book, *Reading Scripture as the Church: Dietrich Bonhoeffer's Hermeneutic of Discipleship* (IVP Academic) brings Bonhoeffer's voice to bear on contemporary conversations about the theological interpretation of Scripture.

Peter Truasheim is a Master of Theology student at BBI-The Australian Institute if Theological Education, Sydney. He has twice won the annual award, Flechtheim Scholarship, for student work that furthers understanding of Bonhoeffer's theology.

CPSIA information can be obtained
at www.ICGtesting.com
Printed in the USA
JSHW031650120320
4695JS00002B/97